A Prairie Memoir

A Prairie Memoir:

The Life and Times of James Clinkskill
1853–1936

Edited by S.D. Hanson

Introduction by S.D. Hanson,
André N. Lalonde and J. William Brennan

Canadian Plains Research Center, 2003

UNIVERSITY OF
REGINA

Canadian Plains Research Center
University of Regina
Regina, Saskatchewan S4S 0A2
Canada
Tel: (306) 585-4758
Fax: (306) 585-4699
e-mail: canadian.plains@uregina.ca
http://www.cprc.uregina.ca
National Library of Canada Cataloguing in Publication Data
Clinkskill, James, 1853-1936
  A prairie memoir : the life and times of James Clinkskill, 1853-1936 /
James Clinkskill ; Stan Hanson, editor.
  (Canadian plains studies 03176290 42)
  Includes index.
  ISBN 0-88977-150-2
1. Clinkskill, James, 1853-1936. 2. Frontier and pioneer life—Saskatchewan. 3.
Northwest Territories—History—1870-1905. 4. Saskatchewan—History—1905-
1945. 5. Mayors—Saskatchewan—Saskatoon—Biography. 6. Saskatoon (Sask.)—
Biography. 7. Businessmen—Saskatchewan—Biography. I. Hanson, Stan. II.
University of Regina. Canadian Plains Research Center. III. Title. IV. Series.
FC3547.26.C54A3 2003   971.24'02'092   C2003-910163-0
F1074.5.S3C54 2003
Cover design by Donna Achtzehner, Canadian Plains Research Center
Printed and bound in Canada by Westcan Printing Group, Winnipeg

Contents

Acknowledgments vi
Introduction vii
Chapter One: Getting Started, 1882 to 1885 1
Chapter Two: Insurrection, April to August 1885 33
Chapter Three: Politics, 1886 to 1899 .63
Chapter Four: Saskatoon, 1899 to 1912 125
Postscript 163
Index 165

Acknowledgments

T O ANYONE WHO KNEW STAN HANSON and his work as an archivist and
historian, his personal interest in the journals of James Clinkskill and
his desire to ensure that they be more widely available will come as no
surprise. These journals constitute a union of two of Stan's greatest interests: the settlement of the Canadian prairies and the important role
played by far-sighted individuals who made it their business to build a
new life for themselves and those who came after them.

We would like to thank a number of individuals who were of great
help to Stan as he prepared this volume. We are particularly indebted to
Stan's dear friend and colleague, André Lalonde, and to Bill Brennan for
his editorial contributions to this book. We would also like to thank
Cheryl Avery, Don Hamilton, Don Kerr, Sandra Lalonde and Patricia
Mathias, who offered Stan their customary support, encouragement and
comments as he worked on this project.

This volume is a tribute to Stan and the work that engaged him
throughout his life. The efforts of his friends and colleagues to ensure
that it was readied for press and published is a tribute of another kind. It
is one for which we, as his family, are most grateful.

Glenys, Melanie and Lawrence Hanson
Saskatoon, Saskatchewan
February 2003

Introduction

THE HISTORY OF SASKATCHEWAN HAS BEEN informed by the diaries, journals and reminiscences of numerous individuals. Many prairie farmers have left a valuable legacy of information relating to weather and climatic conditions, homesteading, farm mechanization, agricultural advances and rural activities. Few urban dwellers have created such records, however, with the result that our knowledge of the experience of pioneer labourers and entrepreneurs is less complete. True, early newspapers frequently provide detailed accounts of events and occurrences but newspapermen often filter the information printed and the chronicles usually pertained to a specific locale only. This is why the reminiscences of James Clinkskill are unique in many ways.

Clinkskill's reminiscences begin in Glasgow, Scotland, and end in Saskatoon, Saskatchewan, 31 years later. In addition to information pertaining to his life and activities in these locations, he recounts his travels back and forth across the Atlantic Ocean and his journeys within Canada. The reminiscences present a vivid and personal picture of the trials and tribulations of travel in the North-West by land and water before and after the coming of the railroads. They provide information on the establishment, growth and development of a number of prairie communities. Clinkskill reports on his business activities and his experiences in dealing with both Native and immigrant customers. We even are able to accompany him on the hustings as he begins his political career.

Clinkskill's reminiscences are the product of a well-educated immigrant who played a prominent role as a businessman and a politician in the Territorial period and the early years of Saskatchewan. He records not only his business and political activities but also provides an account of the actions of his friends, acquaintances and opponents. His reminiscences detail the experiences of one individual at the forefront of the growth and development of the province of Saskatchewan and the city of Saskatoon. He describes the struggle for responsible government, the North-West Rebellion, the evolution of Battleford and Saskatoon, and the founding of a provincial university—not from the sidelines but from the forefront.

A disappointing aspect of Clinkskill's reminiscences is the absence of detail pertaining to his own family and their various activities. Brief and few are the references to either his spouse or children. This is compounded by the dearth of information available in other sources. With the exception of marriage and obituary accounts, and the social "comings and goings" dutifully reported by the Battleford *Herald* and the Saskatoon *Phoenix*, little is known of the personalities and pursuits of the Clinkskill clan. There is some information on the single son, "Tom," killed in World War I, but very little on his mother or seven sisters. Likewise, there is not much direct information on the profitability of Clinkskill's business ventures. Nevertheless, the reminiscences supplement and complement our knowledge and understanding of many of the significant events which shaped Saskatchewan in the latter part of the nineteenth and early twentieth centuries.

James Clinkskill was born to James and Josephine (Michel) on 9 May 1853 in Glasgow, Scotland. His father was an engineer and iron founder and was for many years engaged in the manufacture of textile mill machinery. Son James attended Madras College of St. Andrews after his early education in Glasgow city schools and at age 17 began a three-year apprenticeship in the cotton and yarn business. After working for 10 years in the cotton and yarn industry Clinkskill purchased a grocery store, a business he operated for three years.

An adventurous spirit, accompanied by weariness from the long hours, drudgery and meagre rewards of shopkeeping prompted a change for James Clinkskill. In mid-February 1882, at the age of 28, he left home aboard the Allan Line's *Parisian* out of Liverpool for the North-West

Territories. After arriving in Halifax, he travelled by train via Montréal, Toronto, and Chicago to Winnipeg, which he reached on 16 March. A brief attempt at homesteading quickly convinced him that his future lay elsewhere:

> Amongst the active immigration of the early 1880s were some who not being adapted to farming decided to try their fortune in catering to the newcomers by establishing trading businesses at points remote from the only railway line, the main line of the Canadian Pacific. Two of these were my partner and myself.[1]

Clinkskill's partner was Thomas E. Mahaffy, a young Ontarian who was also interested in the general merchandise business. They formed a partnership and, on the recommendation of a number of Winnipeg businessmen, decided on Prince Albert as a suitable location for their enterprise.

Prince Albert was situated in present-day central Saskatchewan, the area deemed at the time to be the most attractive to would-be settlers. It was readily accessible from Winnipeg, the major trade and distribution centre of the West, either by overland trail via the Touchwood Hills and Fort Carlton or by steamboat via the Red River, Lake Winnipeg and the Saskatchewan River. Clinkskill and Mahaffy were also probably informed by their Winnipeg colleagues that the Canadian Pacific Railway line was to reach Prince Albert in a couple of years. Already word of the proposed route and the Macdonald government's plans for settling the West had prompted an influx of squatters, traders, land speculators and even a few bona fide settlers to take up land along the North Saskatchewan. All of this suggested a bright future for the settlements at Prince Albert, Battleford and Edmonton.

But, at this time there was no rail line crossing the North-West Territories and the entire area that is now Saskatchewan was sparsely populated by Indians, Métis, traders, and cattlemen. It was in this setting that Clinkskill and Mahaffy opened their general store in a rented building.

---

1. "Experiences Conducting a Store in the 1880s," a paper presented to the members of the Saskatoon Historical Society by James Clinkskill. Morton Manuscript Collection 550/1/26.3b, University of Saskatchewan Libraries (Special Collections).

They purchased a stock of goods in Winnipeg and arranged shipment via the Red River and Lake Winnipeg, then up the Saskatchewan River to Prince Albert. The remainder of the stock they brought overland from Troy (now Qu'Appelle). The following October they moved the business to Battleford, opening a store in a small log building on the south side of the Battle River.

> The inducements to our minds were that it was the capital of the North West Territories (in 1883 the capital was moved to Regina). There was a troop of North West Mounted Police there, nearby were several Indian reservations, the headquarters of the Indian Agency, the stores of the Department [of the Interior] were in the village, and a nucleus of settlers. The only places of business were the Hudson's Bay Company and A. Macdonald of Winnipeg. We were optimistic enough to think we could get enough trade to make it pay.[2]

Obtaining goods for sale or trade and their pricing were complicated undertakings, as Clinkskill describes:

> All our goods came by rail to Swift Current, a divisional point on the CPR, situated two hundred miles from Battleford. This place was a small hamlet consisting of one general store and a few shacks housing railway employees. From thence the goods were transported in carts to Battleford. The loading of the goods was a particular job, each piece had to be weighed separately for two reasons. The first was that the freighters were desirous of getting paid for every pound loaded and the second was to enable them to balance the load properly so that there was no heavy weight on the back of the pony.
>
> It was wonderful to see how carefully the pieces were tightly packed to prevent friction of one piece against another during the shaking going over the prairie trail. The loads varied from six hundred to a thousand pounds each cart according to the strength of the pony. These freighters were almost entirely Half-breeds who had for years transported goods for the Hudson's Bay Company. It was a rare thing for us to complain of damages during transit, much less than the damage by rail, and there was a total absence of pilfering. One cause

---

2. Ibid.

of damage for which we could not hold the freighters [responsible] was that done by field mice. Should a brigade be delayed on the road and compelled to camp for a few days, the mice would get into the cases or bales and nibble at the goods. I have had the experience in unpacking a package of overalls to find that the mice had nibbled the folded ends completely across the bundle and in holding up the garment was seen a clean-cut opening where no opening should be. A piece of silk folded in the usual manner had the selvedge eaten away or a hole in a sack of flour leaving a white stream on the trail. These damages had all to be added to the cost of transportation.

The rate we paid at first was four dollars per hundred pounds; later as competition became keen the price was lower till in the 1890s, when we could get our goods to Saskatoon (ninety miles from Battleford) by rail, the rate had decreased to two dollars per hundred pounds. There was never any difficulty in obtaining freighters as these people had no other means of livelihood and during the season, April to October, they kept continually on the trail. During the winter months, after the snow had fallen, it was hard to get them to travel except at exorbitant rates. We had to buy in large quantities, forecasting for six months' trade at least.

After the goods arrived at Battleford there was the task of properly calculating the total cost of transportation, rail and overland. Each case or bale had to be figured separately. Each item of the contents had to be weighed, the tare and cost of the case (no pasteboard containers then) added to find the rate per pound. The rail and overland rate added together would approximate nine or ten cents per pound. The rate being ascertained, each article or a number of the same articles had the net cost of transportation added to the original cost. Each article or garment had a ticket on it stating the cost in code and the selling price in plain figures. The first was required in making up the inventory, the other was to guide our assistants, some of whom had weak "memories." This meticulous costing was necessary. In the same case there might be some goods of low value but heavy in weight and others of high value in proportion to weight. Each had to bear its legitimate cost of transportation.

After getting the goods unpacked and the cost ascertained, the next thing was to sell them. Currency was notably scarce, in fact for small amounts—15¢, 25¢, and 50¢—we adopted (after the example of one of our competitors) issuing our own paper money for these amounts, silver money being scarce. When trading we had to take in payment any kind of produce which we could afterwards dispose of—grain, cattle, beef, fish and milk frozen in the winter time, cordwood, charcoal for blacksmith use, lime, Seneca root, and furs.[3]

Mail service, like freighting, played a pivotal role in the operation of a general store in the North-West Territories in the 1880s and 1890s. In addition to bringing news of family and friends, the mail service brought information on the availability and costs of goods, as well as provision for certain financial and banking services. Like freighting, it also provided a unique form of passenger service, according to Clinkskill:

In 1876 when preparations were being made by the government to establish the capital, the carrying of the Saskatchewan mail was arranged for. This mail was to leave Winnipeg once every three weeks for all points west, outside of the boundary of Manitoba, via Fort Pelly, Humboldt, Duck Lake, Carleton, Battleford, and then direct to Edmonton. The trip from Winnipeg to Edmonton was to be accomplished in twenty-three days.

The Saskatchewan mail contract was let for $1000.00 a trip and at least seventeen trips had to be made in one year. Passenger fare to Battleford was $75.00 and "grub" themselves. They were allowed to carry one hundred pounds of luggage free, including their bedding, and the rest was carried at prevailing rates which varied from three to four-and-a-half dollars a half-hundred, according to the state of the roads. This extra luggage was delivered as soon as possible, which might be three months hence. Tickets for farther west were higher in proportion to the distance. On account of the glorious uncertainty as to when the left-behind baggage might reach its destination, passengers used to invent schemes for carrying as much as possible with them. One old gentleman,

_____

3. Ibid.

who had been the object of pity on the entire trip because of the difficulty he experienced in getting about, on reaching his destination took off three suits of clothes and two overcoats which he had worn on the trip. A lady passenger later folded a sufficient number of clothes to make a good pillow and by sewing them in a calico slip was able to get them through with her.

It was the custom for the mail to stop at every Hudson's Bay Company post to deliver its packet and receive mail for other places. The hospitality extended to travellers has been handed down as part of the history of the West. Stopping-places were built on the route to accommodate the men and their horses for the night. Sometimes it was a log structure in some ravine or, as on the edge of the Salt Plain, a dugout. Wherever it was, a clay fireplace was built in one corner and wood was cut at nearest bluff and carried on the load to provide the night's fire. Hay was cut in its season and stacked for the use of the mail service.

The diet *en route* was mostly pemican and fish, as the latter was easily packed while frozen, and in later years bacon, beans, and molasses contributed largely to the bill of fare. Of course the meals at the Hudson's Bay posts were always of the best and embraced all the varieties of fowl and meat with which the prairies so liberally abounded. On reaching camp each group of travellers prepared their own meals. Frequently one man more handy than the rest was told off as cook and exempted from the work of looking after the horses and other outside work. Occasionally meals could be obtained at the homes of some of the settlers on the route at fifty cents apiece, with an extra charge of twenty-five cents for spreading your blankets on the floor.

Travellers on the prairies grew to be great tea drinkers, for a halt was made every four hours to rest and feed the horses. This was called a "spell." A fire was always built and a kettle of tea made from which all partook although nothing was eaten except at proper meal hours. Possibly one reason for this was that the water from a slough was all that could be had and it was necessary to boil it to be healthy, and in the winter the snow had to be melted to procure water on the plains.

After 1878 Battleford was the seat of the government for the Territories, and its residents awaited the arrival of the mails with eagerness. As the time varied anywhere from ten to eighteen days after its despatch from Winnipeg the esteemed postmaster and telegraph operator, Hugh Richardson, used to hoist the Union Jack by day and a lantern by night as a signal that Her Majesty's mail had arrived. This meant a general rush to the post office and the town assumed a sort of holiday appearance as good news, official news, and news and the contents of the newspapers were duly discussed by all concerned.

As the railways opened up the country the mails were carried as far as possible by rail and met there by the new contractor's teams. In summers the mail rigs were strong democrat-wagons, which would carry the mail and from two to five passengers. In the fall of 1882 the mail went from Qu'Appelle every two weeks. When the Canadian Pacific railway had completed its line to the coast the Battleford mail struck off from Swift Current while the Edmonton mail left from Calgary. This contract was to be for a mail every ten days and later once a week. When the Canadian Northern Pacific built its line into Prince Albert, Saskatoon was made the starting point for the mail with a trip weekly service, and eventually, after the main line was completed to Edmonton, Battleford enjoyed the luxury of a daily mail.[4]

A few years after his leaving Prince Albert, serious trouble erupted near Clinkskill's former location. The Métis of the district, whose many grievances had been ignored for years by the government in Ottawa, suddenly faced a repeat of the land survey system which had provoked many of them to leave Red River for the banks of the North and South Saskatchewan rivers where they settled on river lots, as favoured by their Québec ancestors. Many of these Métis, who had previously established themselves as buffalo hunters, fur traders, freighters and guides, had settled at Batoche and created a number of successful businesses which ultimately expanded to St. Laurent, Duck Lake, Prince Albert, and other

---

4. "The Route and Routine of the Saskatchewan Mail in Pioneer Days," a paper by James Clinkskill (probably for presentation to the Saskatoon Historical Society). Morton Manuscript Collection 550/1/26.5, University of Saskatchewan Libraries (Special Collections).

northern communities. Now, in the early 1880s the Canadian government was ignoring the river lot system and replacing it with a rectangu-
lar grid pattern which took no account of existing land holdings. It was
too much. The Métis already had had to relocate, adapt their lifestyle
and adjust to the onslaught of an alien society that plowed and fenced
the land, sowed and harvested crops and otherwise altered a previous
existence. And, now, the survey.

The failure of the federal government to adequately address the grievances of the Métis eventually led to an armed confrontation with the
North-West Mounted Police at Duck Lake on 26 March 1885. Although
there was loss of life on both sides, it was the killing of a dozen policemen
which was featured in the headlines of the East's newspapers. Cries for
vengeance and a demand for the end of the lawlessness of the West did
not go unheeded. Prime Minister Macdonald now reacted quickly and
within days more than 5,000 regular troops, militiamen and volunteers
were mobilized. A force of this size was deemed necessary in view of the
possibility of many of the North-West Territories' 20,000 Indians rising up
in support of their Métis brethren.

The Indians who had surrendered lands in the North Saskatchewan
River region under Treaty 6, one of a series of similar treaties negotiated
with the western bands between 1871 and 1877, were as unhappy as the
Métis. They, too, were alarmed by the encroachment of a white civilization that threatened their customs and traditions and a distant government that restricted their movements, controlled their food source and
otherwise altered their way of life. In the very recent past there had been
confrontations between these Treaty Indians and the government's farm
instructors, agents and other representatives. Even before the North-
West Field Force reached the area, there was more trouble. On 2 April
members of Big Bear's Cree band attacked the village of Frog Lake and
killed a number of its inhabitants. The North-West Rebellion was under-
way and it was conceivable that the Canadian forces would face an
enemy that outnumbered them several to one.

Clinkskill enlisted in the volunteer Home Guards during the 1885
Métis Rebellion and was under arms for 60 days, awaiting the arrival of
the Canadian troops. "The alarm began with the fight at Duck Lake and
the Battleford police post, from which most of the mounted police had

been promptly moved to Prince Albert, was prepared for a siege."[5] The 400 "beleaguered pioneers of Battleford," consisting of approximately 100 men and 300 women and children, were quartered in the stockade, located across the river from the town, throughout the 24-day siege. Although no direct attack was made on the fort, many houses and buildings in the town were looted and burned. Clinkskill's own home and store were ransacked and his principal store was razed. The inhabitants of Battleford and district, who were confined to the fort for most of the period of unrest, were kept informed by telegraph and word of mouth of the various confrontations with the Indians and Métis. Many lived in constant fear that they, too, would suffer the fate of the people of Frog Lake.

After the rebellion Clinkskill and Mahaffy enlarged their "secondary" store and erected a new storehouse on a location in the Battleford town site. Business was brisk as everyone had to restock after the loss of their goods during the rebellion. The Clinkskill-Mahaffy partnership was amicably dissolved in 1896, however, when Mahaffy decided to leave the business. Then in June 1899, Clinkskill purchased the small establishment of James Leslie and J.R. Wilson in Saskatoon. When the CPR was rerouted across the southern region of the Territories, Battleford languished, but Clinkskill retained his mercantile interests there until February 1908, at which time he decided to "slow down" and to concentrate on his Saskatoon businesses.

In addition to his dedication to his business interests, Clinkskill devoted time to his personal and social life. In 1884 he journeyed to Winnipeg where he married Dora Babington Taylor, originally of Brantford, Ontario. This union produced eight offspring: Dora ("Doll," 1885–1979), Margaret (1887–?), James ("Tom," 1889–1916),[6] Grace

---

5. *Edmonton Journal*, 16 July 1926, p. 22. For the most recent interpretation of events in Battleford during the Rebellion of 1885 the reader should consult the article written by J.L. Tobias, "Canada's Subjugation of the Plains Cree," *Canadian Historical Review* (1983).

6. James Thomas Clinkskill, a real estate partner with F.A. Giddings, was the first Saskatonian to enlist for World War I. A Captain in the Saskatoon Fusiliers, he was killed in action on 16 September 1916 at the Battle of the Somme after less than a month in the trenches.

(1891–?), Louise ("Burnie," 1895–?), Josephine ("Jo," 1897–1954), Georgina ("Georgie," 1899–1970), and Jean (1902–1932). After a brief stay in a local hotel and temporary residence above the Clinkskill store on Twenty-first Street, the family moved in 1908 into a commodious new home on the corner of Spadina Crescent and Nineteenth Street. Three years later they moved farther up the street, from 152 to 426 Spadina Crescent East and in 1918 to 422 Fourth Avenue North. Mrs. Clinkskill died on 19 September 1917 at age 60. The following August James Clinkskill married Georgina Gibson, originally from Québec and latterly of North Battleford, who predeceased him on 4 March 1932.

Although he was extremely busy with his business and family commitments, he could not resist the pressure of his friends and colleagues to enter the field of politics. In 1888 Clinkskill was elected to the Legislative Assembly of the North-West Territories as the representative for the Battleford district. He served his constituents in this capacity for a period of 10 years, during which he was an active proponent in the cause of obtaining responsible government for the North-West Territories. A series of amendments to the 1869 *An Act for the temporary government of Rupert's Land and the Northwestern Territories when united with Canada* gradually moved the North-West from colonial status to responsible government. Initially, an appointed lieutenant-governor and an advisory council were responsible for the administration of justice and the establishment of institutions and ordinances, subject to ratification by the Canadian Parliament. Subsequent amendments to *The North-West Territories Act* invested the lieutenant-governor and the council with both executive and legislative powers, but not financial control. In 1875 one such amendment provided for the election of members to the council. Once the elected membership reached 21, the council was reconstituted as the Legislative Assembly.[7] Nevertheless, the federal government was

---

7. C. Cecil Lingard, *Territorial Government in Canada* (Toronto: University of Toronto Press, 1946), 3–7. For an authoritative analysis of the political history of the North-West Territories, the reader should consult the book written by L.H. Thomas, *The Struggle for Responsible Government in the North-West Territories, 1870–1897* (Toronto: University of Toronto Press, 1978).

still more than a generation away from granting responsible government to the North-West Territories.

To Clinkskill and many of his colleagues in the territorial legislature, full responsible government equated to "controlling the purse"—they should have full control of both territorial revenues and the annual appropriation from the federal government. According to Clinkskill, it initially appeared the goal had been achieved with ease:

> The supply bill of 1888 had contained every cent of the Dominion grant for government of the Territories. At the close of the session Lieutenant-Governor Royal had declared "The practical sense with which you have met my efforts to take advantage of the present transitory regime, to give you as large a share of responsibility as possible in the administration of the affairs of government of these vast Territories has left me no cause for regret." We considered we had gained full responsible government.
>
> The Ottawa authorities did not approve of the actions of Lieutenant-Governor Royal in giving the Assembly latitude in governmental matters and in 1889, when the next session was held, we very soon found that His Honour intended to act strictly within the letter of the Act of 1888.
>
> The first indication of the change in His Honour's attitude was when he declined to submit to the Assembly a full state-ment of the Public Accounts. The privilege of advising and directing had been accorded in the previous session and when it was withdrawn the Assembly claimed it as a right. On October 29, 1889 the first Advisory Council resigned. Two main reasons were alleged, "grave faults of administration" in which the Lieutenant-Governor had either acted without the advice of the Council or had ignored it, and because we can-not continue to work under a system in which our most important powers are only granted us in the form of conces-sions and because we are unwilling to accept responsibility without a corresponding right of control. The Lieutenant-Governor demanded to know the character of the "grave faults of administration." At the time no answer was given but in the following session, December 1890, [F.W.G.] Haultain, in reviewing the situation, gave a detailed statement of them.

That tenders had been received for a certain portion of printing and His Honour had not let the contract for some time after and for reasons the Council did not deem-sufficient.

That a certain member of the House was refused payment of one hundred dollars for expenses of an immigration agent to the East.

That the late Mr. R. Dundas Strong of Qu'Appelle was retained as counsel in an important case after the Advisory Council had recommended his services be dispensed with.

That the Public Accounts report was not submitted to the Council before being laid on the table of the House.

That in the case of a contract given by Lieutenant-Governor Dewdney to one Whitford to build a bridge over the Blind Man River, when the contractor failed before the contract was finished His Honour had paid claims of certain creditors before waiting to advertize for all of the creditors as the Council had advised.

On November 5th, a week after the resignation of the first Advisory Council, the Lieutenant-Governor selected a new one. … This new Council issued a statement declaring that it would exercise "the functions of an executive in matters affecting the Territorial finances only as well as discharge the duties assigned to the Lieutenant-Governor-in-Council."

Without consulting the Assembly, solely on the invitation of the Lieutenant-Governor, the new Council had acquiesced in the position that it was not such an executive. It had surrendered a right which its predecessor had both claimed and exercised.[8]

During his 10 years' service in the Assembly (1888–1898), Clinkskill saw responsible government won for the North-West Territories. In a 1903 by-election he again was elected to the Legislative Assembly where he served until 1905 as the representative for the Saskatoon district.

---

8. "The Struggle for Responsible Government in the North West Territories," a paper by James Clinkskill (probably for presentation to the Saskatoon Historical Society). Morton Manuscript Collection 550/1/26.2, University of Saskatchewan Libraries (Special Collections).

Although politics played an important role in his life, Clinkskill never neglected the chief source of his livelihood, his private businesses. Shortly after his arrival in Saskatoon, Clinkskill had a two-storey addition built onto the store he had purchased from Leslie and Wilson. He remained at this location (later that part of the Queen's Hotel on Twentieth Street fronting on First Avenue) until 1906, when he sold the property to D. Kennedy. In 1903 Clinkskill purchased three lots south of his First Avenue location on which he built a grain warehouse and photographic studio. That same year he also purchased four lots on the corner of First Avenue and Twenty-first Street, later the site of the Ritz Hotel and the Royal Bank, from John Braithwaite. Ignoring the counsel of many of his fellow citizens, who attempted to dissuade him from building at a location so distant from the established business district, Clinkskill moved into his new store in 1907:

> The store is a substantial cement edifice, quite characteristic of the stability and thrift displayed by the commercial men of the city. A departmental trade is conducted, and employment given to fifteen or twenty men. On the ground floor are hardware, dry goods, gents' furnishings and groceries, while the second floor is taken up with a cafe and a splendid display of ladies' clothing, dressmaking and a large assortment of glassware. A ladies' waiting room has already been installed. There is a large basement the full length of the building, which is used for storage purposes. The store is one of the largest and most imposing in the city.[9]

Once the post office and Canadian Northern Railway station were erected next door, Clinkskill's store was no longer the only establishment on Twenty-first Street between First and Second Avenues and it soon became one of the most valuable properties in Saskatoon. Clinkskill built his new home and store just a few years before Saskatoon entered its boom period.

Prior to his retirement in 1923, Clinkskill owned a general store, grain warehouse, and photographic studio. He also was a director of J.C.

---

9. *Saskatoon Capital* (Anniversary Number), June 1909.

Drinkle's company in Saskatoon and, together with James Leslie and J.F. Cairns, owned a cement block company.

Clinkskill brought his political and governmental experience from the territorial arena to the municipal sphere when he was elected mayor of Saskatoon in 1905. On 1 July 1906 he gained the distinction of being the last mayor of the town and the first mayor of the city. Effectively the author of Saskatoon's city charter, in this and a subsequent term as the chief executive of the municipality (1911 and 1912) Clinkskill oversaw major advances in and extension of civic services in Saskatoon. Between 1910 and 1913, a period during which he served a second stint as mayor, everything went up and up and up. The population almost trebled, to 28,000; building permits increased by more than $6 million to over $7.75 million; assessment jumped from $8 million to almost $37 million; and the number of real estate firms grew from 37 in 1909 to 267 in 1912, all of them attempting to sell lots in over 100 subdivisions.[10] Clinkskill himself enjoyed some profitable real estate dealings during the boom.

While a resident of Battleford, Clinkskill had chaired the local school board between 1888 and 1898, and shortly after his arrival in Saskatoon he was elected a school trustee. When the University of Saskatchewan was founded in 1907, it seemed only fitting that he should be appointed to the Board of Governors of the new institution. Upon the expiry of his initial term of office, Clinkskill was elected to the University Senate and named its representative on the Board. In addition to being appointed to the Board of Governors, he served as its chairman from 1911 to 1925. Once again, as with the early development of the city, Clinkskill was intimately involved in establishing what is today one of the most attractive university campuses in the country.

Throughout his career in Saskatoon, Clinkskill was recognized as a tireless booster of the city and its business community. He was equally committed to a number of the city's charitable organizations and fraternal societies. Together with James R. Wilson, he was involved in the creation of the Associated Charities, a pre-war charity established to assist

10. Don Kerr and Stan Hanson, *Saskatoon: The First Half-Century* (Edmonton: NeWest Press, 1982), 105.

xxii A Prairie Memoir: The Life and Times of James Clinkskill

the poor of Saskatoon. He played a prominent role in the founding of the Patriotic Fund, the first wartime charity to provide for soldiers' dependents, and was the prime organizer of the Fathers of Volunteers Association and the Returned Soldiers' Welcome and Aid League. A Conservative in politics and a Presbyterian in religion, Clinkskill was president of the St. Andrew's Society, a member of the Independent Order of Odd Fellows and the Knights of Pythias, and a charter and life member of the Masonic Lodge A.F. and A.M. No. 16. When he died on 6 August 1936, after a brief illness, Lodge No. 16 conducted the graveside service.

In editing and preparing these reminiscences for publication, every effort has been made to allow James Clinkskill to tell his own story. Where additional information, clarification or corrections are required, these are added in the footnotes. Clinkskill's reminiscences, prepared in 1917, are informed by certain private documents, newspaper articles, and entries in the *Journals of the Legislative Assembly of the North-West Territories*. However, some passages which contained widely known information or which tended to impede the flow of the narrative have been deleted, such as a genealogy of the Mackay family, two lengthy articles from the *Saskatchewan Herald*, and several extensive quotations from the *Journals*. Because the reminiscences were an initial draft,[11] typographical, punctuation, and spelling errors have been corrected without using [sic], as is favoured by some editors. James Clinkskill was an educated, knowledgeable, and articulate gentleman quite capable of performing most of the amendments which appear in this version of his life and career.

---

11. Copies are held in the Local History Room, Saskatoon Public Library, the University of Saskatchewan Libraries (Special Collections), and the Saskatchewan Archives Board. Excerpts have appeared in the Saskatoon *Star-Phoenix*, *Gargoyle*, and other publications.

Chapter One:
Getting Started, 1882 to 1885

IN 1881 REPORTS REACHED US IN GLASGOW, SCOTLAND, where I lived of the wonderful new country being opened up in Manitoba. These reports gave rise to many discussions regarding the opportunities offered there for young men in various branches of industry. At that time little mention was made of the vast undeveloped stretches of country west of Manitoba; attention was concentrated on that province only. At the meetings of a coterie of young men held weekly in the premises of a tobacconist in Sauciehall Street, called the "School," the subject was frequently discussed by us. Then, as now, it was contended that in Britain all lines of business were so fully developed by concerns commanding large resources that young men with limited capital had very little chance of succeeding in business. The members were fairly representative of various lines of business. One was in a timber merchant's employ, another a clerk in a railway company office, another in the city gas office, two were sons of an iron founder (these two were settled in their father's business so the emigrating ideas did not appeal to them) and the others were employed in offices of various branches of trade. At that time I was conducting a grocery business at Bridgeton Cross in the east end of Glasgow. The work was strenuous, from seven in the morning till eight at night during the week except Saturday, when it was twelve o'clock before closing up. The average purchase per customer running about eight cents, it can easily be imagined that there was drudgery connected with it.

One night in November, after a heated controversy, I decided to go out to Manitoba and see for myself I acquainted my parents with my decision. It took a little time to dispose of my business and wind up my affairs. In January 1882 I was ready to take my departure. About the middle of February I sailed on the Allan liner *Parisian*, then a new ship, from Liverpool. Three years previous to this time two of my former school mates at St. Andrews, sons of a farmer, had gone to Manitoba. I intended looking them up.

On the ship I foregathered with some young men going out like myself to try their fortune. We agreed to travel together to our destination. On arriving at Halifax our luggage was so late in being landed from the ship that we had to wait over till the next day. It took the train 42 hours to go 843 miles; the snow was deep, in some places being piled as high as the top of the cars. We found it strange travelling in open coaches, accustomed as we were to the compartment style of carriages. It was very trying to sit up all night in the seat and no sooner getting asleep when some brakeman would shout the next stopping place, or a conductor would demand our tickets for examination. At last we reached Montreal. A fellow passenger recommended a hotel at which we stayed. It was a very unsatisfactory place; dirty was no word for it. We were amused at the smoke pipes from the stoves wandering underneath the ceiling in a sinuous course to the chimney, a system of heating new to us. As we had been accustomed at home, we left our shoes outside the door to be polished. In the morning we had difficulty in finding them; someone had kicked the shoes all into a heap at the end of the passage. On our remonstrating with them, we were informed that shoe cleaning was not included in the service but had to be arranged for with an extra charge for a shine. After staying a few days in Montreal we went on to Toronto. Our next stop was in Chicago where we saw for the first time cable streetcars.

In Chicago, on going to a ticket office to find out about the station we had to leave from, the man in charge, after examining our tickets, emitted a stream of oaths the like of which I had never heard. It seemed his outburst was occasioned by finding that we had been routed by the most roundabout route possible between Chicago and St. Paul. However, we had to bear with it. After our experience in getting to St. Paul we did not wonder so much at his awful blasphemy. From St. Paul to Winnipeg we travelled by the St. Paul and Manitoba Railway. Along this line the land was level on both sides of the track and, for the greater part of the way, water covered the prairie on both sides for as far as the eye could see. There had been during the preceding winter heavy falls of snow which had now melted with the approach of spring and, there being no slopes to drain off the water, it lay deep on the land.

On the night of 16th March we arrived in Winnipeg. We had difficulty in finding a place to stay as every hotel was filled to overflowing. At last we got track of a place called the Club Hotel at the south end of Main Street just about opposite the Hudson's Bay store. What a joint it was! Two of us in a room about nine by ten, dark and stuffy. The windows were sealed airtight and evidently had not been cleaned for years. The water supplied for washing was discoloured, showing a dark sediment at the bottom of the jug. The meals offered us at breakfast the next morning were repulsive and we began to have doubts of our wisdom in coming to such a country. Next day, after parading around and having got some friends to use influence, we got into the Canadian Pacific hotel, a building on the opposite side of Main Street, where it was clean anyway. This was a building formerly used by the Hudson's Bay Co. for housing their employees.

On our arrival in Winnipeg we had our first experience of riding in a sleigh. It was an omnibus body mounted on runners. The ride from the station to the hotel was a constant succession of jolts. The snow had been deep and was worn down into hollows, evidently following the ruts that had been left in the mud when the freeze-up came. To say that we enjoyed the ride was wide of the mark; we simply "tholed"[1] it as the Scottish expression is. The city was crowded with strangers from all parts. The great land boom was then at its height. Real estate offices were everywhere. In the hotel rotundas crowds were gathered, bartering lots, buying and selling lots. Transactions of large amounts were made, the only record being perhaps a memorandum on a bit of wrapping paper!

---

1. To undergo or suffer pain.

Auction sales were being held day and night of lots in new town sites. One particularly I remember was Rapid City, a very small place today. Lots were being sold in and around that place for miles out. Nelsonville was another; Emerson lots seemed to be in demand; Brandon and Portage la Prairie were prime favourites; Point Douglas lots were considered good; and Fort Rouge was just being opened up. One auctioneer, Scones I think his name was, seemed to be most successful in stirring up enthusiasm. Farm lands in Manitoba were changing hands, ten and twelve dollars an acre being considered a high price. There were farm lands being offered by holders of Half-breed scrip[2] at very low prices, which tended to keep down the average price.

As there was great demand for men to go on survey parties, some of our party hired on and went off on the prairie. Not hearing from my friends I made enquiry how to get to them. I found that by going to Emerson by rail and then taking stage to Nelsonville, I could get within a few miles of their farm. I determined to go, leaving my heavy baggage till I should return. I got to Emerson, a chilly, bleak-looking town and stayed overnight at a miserable little hotel at West Lyne. I started off in the morning on the stage, a big open sleigh, completely filled with passengers.

Before leaving Winnipeg I was strongly advised to buy a pair of moc-casins. Money could not buy a pair of overshoes or rubbers in Winnipeg! After hunting through innumerable stores I eventually found a pair of what they called "Squaw moccasins."[3] This footgear I carefully placed over my leather boots! As they were too small for me they compressed my feet, making my suffering from cold intense. When we got out a few miles, a severe snowstorm started with a bitterly cold wind blowing in our faces which soon became a regular blizzard. Having the old-countryman's

---

2. Scrip was a certificate issued to Métis entitling the bearer to 240 acres or money for the purchase of land, issues in compensation for lands lost by the Métis after the North-West Rebellion. Note that the term "Half-breed," which Clinkskill uses throughout this book, while inappropriate today, was not considered offensive in Clinkskill's day.

3. Note that the term "squaw," which Clinkskill occasionally uses when referring to a woman of First Nation ancestry, while inappropriate today, was not considered offensive in Clinkskill's day.

indispensable umbrella along with me, I hoisted it trying to protect my face from the sharp blasts of snow. Very soon I had to close it as I found it too cold on my hands to hold it up. I had no mittens, simply a pair of woolen gloves, almost no better than bare hands.

Our progress was diversified by frequent upsets of the sleigh. There had been so much travel on this route that the road was higher than the prairie on each side. The horses, floundering along, would get off the high ridge and would go over into the snow. About three o'clock in the afternoon we reached Brown's stopping house. This place was crowded with people. Many of them had been there for several days, not daring to start out on account of the snow and bad roads. Our party was very hungry, not having eaten since early morning at Emerson. Nothing could persuade the proprietor to give us anything to eat till the regular hour for a meal at six o'clock, but you could have anything you liked to drink if you had the price!

When the meal was ready there was a general stampede for a place at the table, the dining room being so small that there were three sittings before all were accommodated. At night we had to sleep two in a bed and such a bed! The bed clothes seemed to have had a very distant interview with a tub. The glass in the windows of the little room I slept in was coated with ice about an inch thick, there being no storm windows.

Next day we started out for Crystal City, following some others who had started out early breaking the road for us. At noon we stopped at a Mennonite's house. Here I had a new experience. We entered through the stable into the living room which was heated by a large brick flue running lengthwise of the room. The fuel was dried cow manure mixed with straw which made a peculiar musky smell. The only food they could give us was boiled eggs. No bread, no bannock, no salt even, simply plain boiled eggs. I was at a loss as to how to get the egg disposed of so that it would appease my hunger. There were no spoons or other table requisites so I took a look to see how the others who were more at home in a predicament like this would act. They knocked off the shell all round and then bolted the eggs in one gulp! I thought it was a terribly savage way to eat but since then many times have I been situated when a meal of eggs bolted holus-bolus would have looked like a banquet. The hotel at

Crystal City was not bad so we stayed over night. The next day we made Nelsonville. By good chance one of my Scottish friends happened to be in the town for supplies. We drove out in the afternoon to the farm.

I resided with my friends till the beginning of May when I joined a party going west to take up homesteads. Driving into Emerson we encountered lots of water but the bottom on the trail was good, as the ground was not thawed out yet, and we made good progress. I imagine the road would be nearly impassable after the frost had come out of the ground. At Emerson the Red River was in flood and there was no crossing on the bridge. We got over on a steamer that ferried us over, landing some passengers on the second floor of the hotel and the others on the railway embankment. Taking the train, I arrived at Winnipeg. (Amongst the archives at my former home in Scotland, was found recently a diary I had kept and sent to my folks at home of the trip we were just starting on. I will give it in part.)

> We left Winnipeg for Brandon on the 12th May 1882 intending to get supplies and thence proceed to Pipestone Creek to take up government land which was already on the market. The company consisted of four persons, Jim, Jack, Dick, and myself. We got to Brandon about eight o'clock at night, it having taken us about twelve hours to go 145 miles. The trains in this country did not travel at great speed; the track was too slimly and cheaply laid to admit of swift running. It consisted of a little grading or raising of the earth, the rails laid on sleepers or ties with a spike driven in on each side, and with no chairs or wedges being used. The result looked strange to me as I was accustomed to seeing the substantial lines of the old country railways. Looking along the line the eye could follow the wavy lines of the steel, suggesting a serpent in repose. This was the Canadian Pacific Railway just being constructed. We passed a trainload of settlers' effects that had run off the track and the cars were lying side up in about eight feet of water. Next morning we inquired at the land office about vacant sections. We decided to go out west and squat on land not yet on the market as in this way we thought of getting a better selection of good land. The district we decided to make for was north of Moose Mountain.

At Brandon we found oxen so scarce and expensive that it was arranged for Jim and Jack to go back to Winnipeg and buy oxen, wagons, and supplies and ship them by rail to Flat Creek (now Oak Lake), 37 miles west of Brandon. This was carried out and on the 20th May we arrived at Flat Creek after a slow and dangerous journey. Our car was on a siding and was sent against a lot of cars loaded with railway timbers, sending our goods and selves right on top of the oxen and, as we found out afterwards, damaging one of the wagons and the cookstove. As soon as possible we set to work unloading the car and getting the wagons put together. The implements consisted of two ploughs, a mower, a horse, rake, spades, shovels, hayforks, saws, axes, logging chains, etc. Our provisions consisted of flour, oatmeal, bacon, tea, sugar, dried apples, and a few sundries such as soap, candles, etc. It took us all Saturday afternoon and evening to unload the stuff and put the wagons together. On Sunday morning we had to make a platform of railway ties to get out the oxen. The railway men would give us no assistance loading or unloading the car; all the work had to be done by ourselves. On Saturday night a bad snowstorm came with a high wind and extremely cold temperature. A pail of water inside the tent had an inch of ice on top in the morning. Hearing there were some boarding tents where meals could be had, we patronized one of them and got a forty cent meal worth, I should say, about fourpence at a cooking depot in Glasgow.

Monday, 22nd May 1882

After striking camp we got started about eleven o'clock. We had gone a few yards when one of the hames on one of the ox collars gave way, split right through. These were bought new in Winnipeg and had not been used before. After patching it up with twine we got started again, passed through several soft places successfully, and got onto a stretch of sandhills. The trail was dry here but the wheels sank four to six inches in the sand, making the draught on the wagons stiff for the oxen. We camped about six o'clock beside a pond where there was some good grass for the cattle. We were much disappointed at the poor feed; the spring was backward and cold, the grass was poor, and our oxen suffered in consequence. We had the frog chorus in our ears all night. The noise these frogs made was something wonderful; it sounded like a regiment of policemen with all their whistles going together. It was kept up continually, night and day. After a while one got accustomed to it.

Tuesday, 23rd May

We got started at six o'clock. A sandy trail for two miles and then we struck an alkali flat about half a mile wide and extending for miles right across the trail. When we got to the edge of the flat we saw four teams stuck in trying to cross. After a careful reconnoiter of the ground we put both yoke of oxen onto one wagon and started. After floundering to within three or four yards of the hard ground on the other side, the wagon, up to the hubs, became immovable. It being camping time, we pitched our tent and after a meal held a council of war. It seemed impossible for us to go on with the heavy loads we had on our wagons. We decided that two of us should go on about five miles to Gopher Creek (where we were told there was a settler in a log house), taking part of our load to leave there and then come back and divide the balance of our freight between the two wagons. At last we got to sleep after a very exhausting day's work.

Wednesday, 24th May

At three a.m. the wagon started off, returning about ten in the forenoon. We loaded up, the load on the two wagons much lightened by the stuff already taken forward. We reached Gopher Creek in the afternoon. We had to carry part of our load across the railway bridge in order to relieve the weight in our wagons in crossing the creek. These railway bridges were built of beams supported on piles with tiles laid on the beams without any filling between. In walking across we had to be careful not to fall through between the ties.

Thursday, 25th May

In driving the first wagon through the creek, it stuck fast in the mud and caused us great delay. After a deal of pulling and shoving we got it across. We all got wet but as this occurred frequently we did not think anything of it. About three miles further on we arrived at a farm. As our stock of bread had run out, we got one of the farmer's daughters to bake us some. We gave her two dollars and we supplied the flour. Here we left the mower, rake, and our large boxes of clothing, etc., they being the heaviest part of the load. The boxes we put on pieces of logs and covered them up; the farmer promised to look after them. We set off again, camping alongside an old pioneer driving a Red River cart. These carts are of peculiar construction, made wholly of wood—no iron about it. When they are in motion the axles give out most ear-piercing noises as they run in wooden bushings without any grease. The carts suit the roads and I noticed get on faster than our wagons. The wheels are broad and made with a big dish that keeps them from sinking in the muck. The Half-breeds and traders used them for transporting goods and furs long distances. This pioneer was an Ontario man who had been working on the railway for a year and was now on his way to take up a half-section of land. He had saved three hundred dollars and was going to make a start farming.

Friday, 26th May

We made good progress through rolling prairie without any timber, not even scrub. The trail being good, we got on very well.

Saturday, 27th May

We started at 4:30 and made good progress. We crossed two creeks in the afternoon. In trying to jump across one I got in the water up to my waist. We came on a plain of alkali extending about six miles. Carefully avoiding former mistakes, we took the most travelled road and got through without getting stuck. Daily we met teams on their way back, reporting Moose Mountain district to be poor land full of stones, etc. This further depressed our spirits but we determined to push on and see for ourselves. One of our party shot two chickens and a duck. Ducks were plentiful along the trail. We camped at six p.m., oxen very tired.

Sunday, 28th May

Necessary to push on as we had no firewood to cook with. Last evening the pioneer found he was on the wrong trail for his destination so he had to turn back. We camped alongside a bluff of small timber and cooked our game. Here we had a general wash up of sox, etc., which was much needed. The mud seemed to get through into our boots, although they were long ones up to the knee.

Monday, 29th May

We made an early start. The wagon tongue gave way again which delayed our progress. Today we met a lot of Ontario men turning back and making for Qu'Appelle, two hundred miles west. In the afternoon we got on the wrong trail and, the oxen being tired, we camped and got supper made.

Tuesday, 30th May

In breaking camp I always took a good look around. I found we were continually forgetting to pick up something and were missing some of the things badly. On the other hand, in passing old camp grounds we often found things that had been left by other parties who had stopped there. We were beginning to accumulate quite a number of lanterns, etc. We started off at six a.m., retraced our way, and got on the right trail. We had a terribly hard time today. We stuck twice in sloughs and had to unload both times. We met a party of Englishmen turning back and making for Qu'Appelle. They had got to Pipestone Creek, on the trail to Moose Mountains, and seeing the difficulty of crossing the creek they funked it and turned tail. In the afternoon we crossed the railroad track at a siding which is now the site of the town of Moosomin. The mosquitoes were very numerous and troublesome. One of our party, an Englishman, caught a dragon fly which he sent home as a specimen of a North-West mosquito.

Wednesday, 31st May

We arrived at Pipestone Creek about noon. It looked a formidable stream. We had heard stories of the difficulty in crossing, that a man had been drowned shortly before in trying to row across. First we got a wagon box over by paddling and a small rope was taken over. This proved unsatisfactory as the wagon box let in water too freely. Jack and I crossed in the wagon box to lend a hand on the other side. In returning on the box Jack had to swim when it sunk with his weight. He had quite a time getting ashore, his clothes and heavy boots hindering him. On my returning the box sank with me, too, but I held on to the rope and was pulled out. Heavy rain came on so we pitched our tent to keep our stuff dry. Just then a party arrived who gave us a pointer. The tent was put around the outside of the wagon box which helped to keep out some of the water. This party was short of rope so we lent them ours. They allowed us to use their wagon box in getting our stuff ferried over. We stretched a big rope, fastening it to a stump, then pulled it taut. We loaded the goods on boards placed on top of the wagon box and hauling on the rope hand over hand we pulled the load over. We made the oxen swim over. The running gear of the wagons we pulled through the stream and got everything over by sundown. We went to bed, all of us very tired and wet through. One of this party had an overcoat which looked like one that Dick had lost on the trail. After examining it, he found it to be his. He had a great bother to get possession of it. The fellow claimed he had bought it from a man on the trail, paying him two dollars for it. Dick had to pay him the two dollars. We met some terribly hard characters and required to be constantly on our guard.

Thursday, 1st June

After loading up we got along very well till the afternoon when we stuck twice and had to unload on each occasion. One of the oxen was a very stubborn brute, very aggravating. He would pull well through a bad place till nearly out and then select a soft place to lie down. He was a large animal and made a big hole. He managed to so mire himself that he could not pull the load at all. There was nothing for it then but to unhitch, get the cattle on hard ground, and try to yank out the wagon with the logging chains. If that did not succeed we had to unload the freight and pull out the empty wagon and reload it.

Friday, 2nd June

We started at 5:30 a.m. after a cold breakfast. We were without fuel, though a prairie fire was all around us. We halted at midday and attempted to make some pancakes or buns out of our flour and get something we could eat. I attempted to make flapjacks. I got the batter ready, put the bacon grease in the fry pan, but something was wrong with the mixture. When the stuff got good and hot, it boiled up and overflowed onto the fire. We had to fall back on porridge. The mosquitoes were very fierce.

Saturday, 3rd June

We made good time from eight o'clock. Our lunch was cold porridge left over from breakfast and eaten with sugar. We omitted to get syrup in our supplies which would have been acceptable with the porridge. In the afternoon our wagon stuck in the middle of a big pond and the cattle sank in the muck. We had to get out into the waist-high water, unload the wagon, and draw the empty wagon out by hand. We camped soon after in sight of Moose Mountain beside a large party of Ontario, English, and Irish men. Supper consisted of porridge and bacon, without bread.

Sunday, 4th June

Breakfast consisted of oatmeal again. We had to make something in the way of bread or buns fit to eat as I was getting desperate. Oatmeal is good enough in its way but every meal made it become monotonous. After several failures I succeeded in making a sort of biscuit or bun that was actually edible. The feast we had that night. I made enough in my estimation to do us for two or three days but alas, the whole supply disappeared in one meal. As a reward for success in my culinary effort, I was installed as head cook for the rest of the trip.

Monday, 5th June

We passed through some fine land and pleasing scenery. There were wood bluffs with nice ponds of water but the land was too broken for grain farming. We camped on the bank of Swift Creek which was a fine stream, the swiftest running stream of water I ever saw of its size. It was full of fish of which we got a supply; we speared them with a hay fork. We had a good fry which was an acceptable change of diet. We saw others shooting them but as our stock of cartridges was running low we did not use the gun. We all had a fine bath which we enjoyed.

Tuesday, 6th June

We camped at Swift Creek. We looked over adjoining sections and found the good ones all taken up. One wagon went up the mountain for firewood in the afternoon.

Wednesday, 7th June

At 4:30 four of us started out to the west with our empty

wagon along the foot of the mountain and found all the land that was any good taken up. We got a hint to use salt water on the blisters caused by mosquito bites. I tried it and found it gave quite a relief to the itching. These insects are a perfect plague; they bite so much and leave such an itching behind as almost sets one crazy. There was also a small black fly that annoyed one very much. Our sportsman Jack, when we first started out, would not think of shooting a bird unless on the wing but now, when it is a case of providing for the pot and cartridges scarce, he not only shoots at a duck on the water but waits until he gets several in row before firing. What a difference hunger make on a man's sporting proclivities!

Thursday, 8th June

We set out west along the foot of the mountain into Range 5. Two brothers, Irishmen, joined our party today. They had been traveling with an Englishman with whom they had disagreed so they split company and now travel with us. They are sons of an eminent Irish barrister.

Friday, 10th June to Monday, 19th June

We looked around for a suitable location. Jack and a young Canadian near whom we were camping went southeast and found some suitable sections vacant.

Tuesday, 20th June

It rained heavily all day. We cooked a fine fat goose Jack had shot, had a right royal feast, and broached a small keg of "aqua vita" we had been keeping till we should find suitable sections. We had a real good time.

Wednesday, 21st June

Some of the party set out to squat on the sections selected.

Friday, 23rd June

Remainder of the party made off and camped on our locations.

Saturday, 24th June to Monday, 2nd July

We were busy getting ploughing done and erecting a sod house. I tried ploughing but did not make a success of it; my furrows were like the letter "S." On the 28th of June there was a terrific thunderstorm. At Moose Mountain there was thunder all day. This storm was a particularly severe one. The clouds were gathering all day; towards sundown the sky was black. The storm started about 9 o'clock and lasted till 3 in the morning, six hours during which the rain fell in torrents. Our tent which was pitched on sloping ground was flooded inches deep. The lightning was incessant, lighting up the prairie. It seemed to strike and then run along the ground. It played ridge pole, we being in mortal terror while it continued. The sod house we made was not much of a shelter. The walls were only five feet high and made of pieces of turf turned over by the plough and placed on top of each other. To form a roof, poles were placed close together with turf put on top of them. One could not stand upright inside but it made a cool retreat when the sun was hot. When it rained it was misery personified. As it was impossible to dodge the water, one had simply to endure the discomfort of being sodden. This was intended only as a makeshift till a house could be built.

Tuesday, 3rd July

Jack, Dick, one of the Irishmen, and I set off for Flat Creek to get the part of the load we had left at Gopher Creek and to replenish our stock of provisions which was getting low. All went well till we reached Pipestone Creek in which the water had receded. In trying to drive the oxen through the creek with wagons attached, the beasts swayed around and the stream carried them down till stopped by a log laid across. I thought the oxen would drown when their heads got below the log. I crept out on the wagon tongue and released the harness, letting them free. Our provisions were destroyed so we had to go on short commons for a while until we bought some at a contractor's camp near the railway track.

Sunday, 8th July

At the farm where we had left our stuff we found the boxes had been moved from where we had left them. The boxes were uncovered and exposed to the weather; the contents were saturated with water and much destroyed. My folks had supplied me with a generous outfit. There was everything required for housekeeping in the way of bed linen, blankets, tablecloths, etc. These were in a pitiable condition. I spread the stuff out on the grass to get dried, making the prairie look like a bleaching green. Half of the stuff was absolutely ruined with mildew. During the night our oxen broke through a fence and ate up a lot of early potatoes belonging to the farmer. He was wild, threatening to sue us for damages. We did not care as his carelessness in not looking after our boxes cost us a great deal more than his potatoes were worth.

Tuesday, 16th July

Arrived at Flat Creek and had a forty-cent meal, the first square we had for a long time. Jack and the Irishmen went off to Winnipeg to buy supplies. I waited at the camp until they returned, looking after the oxen. I had a weary time of it all by myself.

On the 18th of July we set off for Moose Mountain. We bought a lot more provisions which we got as cheaply as at Winnipeg, taking cost of freight into consideration. We reached Pipestone Creek on the 25th where I left the party. I walked back to the railway track, about eight miles, getting on board a construction train and got into Winnipeg on Wednesday afternoon, the 26th of July.

My sojourn on the prairie convinced me that I was not cut out for farming operations. Being city bred, I was so ignorant of the rudiments of agriculture and I decided it was no use to start learning. It would take too long before I could make any success of it. I determined to try some other way of making a living. Winnipeg had then, I should judge, a population of about 30,000 people. The principal retail business was on Main Street. Shops stretched along from the CPR station to Portage Avenue. The streets were simply trails, no attempt at paving or even efficient grading had been made. When the weather was wet teams had great difficulty getting along; often half a dozen wagons within a short distance would be hub deep in mud. Only a few blocks were built on Portage Avenue, which was the main trail for western travel. This date was just about the height of the great land boom, in fact it was starting on the terrible collapse which is now a matter of history. There were stories of men, multi-millionaires in their own minds, having champagne baths and similar extravagances. A large house was pointed out to me, a regular palace built by one of these men. Alack he could not keep up the pace and never occupied it. I got acquainted with a young man, Tom Mahaffy, from Ontario, who had it in his head to go into the store business. My idea ran in that line, too, so we agreed to combine our capital and start a store. In looking around Winnipeg we found store rents in our estimation so exorbitant that we could not afford to start there. There was a great deal of talk about Prince Albert on the North Saskatchewan as a rising place with a good future before it. The railway was expected to be extended there in two years. We consulted with a lot of business people who professed to know all about it, including the manager of the Commercial Bank to whom I had letters of introduction. We decided to locate there. This banker told us of a store building that could be rented cheaply. We hunted up the owner and signed a lease of it for a year.

The next proposition was how were we to get our goods transported there. It was a long way off. The CPR was running construction trains as far as Troy (now Qu'Appelle station), and from there it was two hundred and eighty miles by trail to Prince Albert. There was also a water route from Selkirk by steamer to Grand Rapids on Lake Winnipeg and then Hudson's Bay steamer up the river to Prince Albert. Unfortunately, we selected the latter route.

We purchased our stock, got it shipped to Selkirk by train and then loaded on a barge which was to be towed by a steamer, the old *Princess* (lately destroyed by fire). We set out with high hopes of reaching the land of promise flowing with milk and honey.

Before leaving Winnipeg I got engaged to be married to Dora Babington Taylor. The affair was to take place after I got settled down to business. As it turned out she did not see Prince Albert till we went on a visit.

There was a delay at Selkirk before sailing and I had here my first look at an Indian. The sight did not remind me of what I had read in Fenimore Cooper's novels. I was introduced to the substitute for tobacco, "*Kin-i-kin-nik*," the inner bark of the red willow, dried and rubbed to a powder. It was vile stuff, catching in the back of the throat and making me gag.

The *Princess* left Selkirk the day after we got on board, down the Red River and out into Lake Winnipeg with the barge in tow. There was quite a merry party on board. Amongst them there were two lawyers, a banker, a journalist, and a doctor all going to locate in Prince Albert, as well as the since eminent politician, T.O. Davis, now a senator. On the way Tom introduced me to "painkiller cocktail," a beverage said to be very popular in the North-West but, excuse me, not anymore for me please! Everything went well till the afternoon of the next day when a big wind got up, making a heavy sea. The captain made for an island, steaming round into the lee side and lay-to, waiting for the storm to abate. This boat was not built for rough weather. It bobbed like a cork on the waves and, with the heavy barge in tow, every time it rose to a wave gave a jerk on the tow line that shook us from stem to stern. And did she roll! I feared sometimes that she would turn turtle. Nearly all the passengers were overcome with seasickness. Some were in mortal terror of shipwreck, lying down anywhere with the life saving jackets on. The sleeping berths were built at right angles to the sides and as the vessel rolled you slid to one end; the next roll you slipped to the other end, making it impossible to have a restful night. I spent the day watching the barge containing our goods and kept figuring out what it would mean should it break loose and get wrecked and all our possessions lost. After a while the wind went down, the sea calming again just as soon as the wind ceased. It is surprising on these small lakes how quickly the sea gets up with a wind and how soon it calms down again.

We arrived at Grand Rapids on Sunday. This was the landing place for Hudson's Bay Company boats. The supplies for the Saskatchewan, Peace River, and Mackenzie districts all went up the Saskatchewan River in steamers belonging to the company. From the wharf the freight was taken on small cars on a tramway drawn by horses to a point three miles away where the post is built. There are a series of rapids on the river, as it flows into Cedar Lake, which prevent boats going up with loads. Everything has to be portaged. At the foot of the falls enormous numbers of white fish are in the eddies. These can be caught by simply dropping in a landing net and scooping them out. Near the post we saw great dogs called huskies. These were tied to trees to prevent them fighting and getting away. They have a look like a wolf and seem to be very fierce. These dogs are used in winter for traveling with flat sleds and each can haul a load of one hundred pounds quite easily. They travel in trains, five dogs generally composing a train with one hitched in front of the other. On the river above the rapids a steamer was being built. The hull had been brought over the lake, dragged up the rapids, and was now being finished with upper works. It was the *Marquis*, a fine boat.

We were chagrined on being told that owing to the low stage of the water in the river the steamer could not go up further than Cumberland House, about half way to Prince Albert. What were we to do? There were two propositions to consider: let the goods go forward and remain at Cumberland House all winter; or ship them back to Winnipeg, forward them by rail to Troy and thence overland by cart to Prince Albert. Figuring the cost of shipping back to Winnipeg, rail freight to Troy, and cartage by land, it was going to add such an enormous cost to the goods that we decided to let them go forward, shipping back to Winnipeg only the perishable goods. After discharging the cargo, the Princess sailed and after an uneventful passage arrived at Selkirk.

Having premises rented at Prince Albert, we had to make some new purchases so as to have something in our store to make expenses. We loaded a car with goods, principally provisions, and shipped it to Troy. The road being under construction and there being no agent at Troy, we had to prepay freight charges and follow the car closely. On arriving at Troy we guarded our car carefully, it being up to us to see that our goods were not stolen, as before shipping we had to sign a release of responsibility. Goods were lying alongside the track that had been dumped out of cars and left exposed to the weather. We engaged an Irishman, Mulholland by name, who had a lot of oxen and carts to freight our goods to Prince Albert. The price we had to pay gave us a shock, four dollars a hundred pounds. He, poor fellow, earned his pay as it was well on in November before he landed at Prince Albert.

The next problem was how were we to get to our destination ourselves. The stage carrying mail and passengers went only once in three weeks. It had just gone and we did not care to wait for the next stage. We bought a little Indian pony and a buckboard and, packing our baggage on it along with a small tent and some provisions, off we started on the long trip. I was totally ignorant of how to handle a horse, not knowing even how to harness one, leaving my partner having to hitch and drive our cayuse. As is usual with those unaccustomed to pony travel, we pushed our little beast too hard the first two days out and consequently it played out on us. Thereafter our progress was slow; we camped often giving the pony lots of time to eat and rest. Traveling through the beautiful Touchwood district we came to the edge of the salt plain and camped for the night. Starting early so as to get across this stretch of barren alkali, by sundown we managed to reach a place where the stage stopped at the only spring of fresh water on the plain. Next afternoon we reached the bluffs on the other side. We did have a roaring fire that night I can tell you. Eight days out we made the South Saskatchewan River, crossed on the ferry at Batoche, and on the twelfth day crawled into Prince Albert. When a few miles from the town we asked how far it was to Prince Albert. The reply we got was that we had been traveling through Prince Albert for some miles! It was a delightful journey from the crossing, passing through woods with nice open spaces and water in ponds all the way along. The town is nicely situated on a level bench along the river, the land sloping up to quite a height on the south and the north bank heavily wooded with spruce timber. We liked the look of the place.

Without difficulty we found the building we had rented. Our hearts went into our boots. The building was of frame, just a shell, unpainted, and a most disreputable looking place. No use crying over spilt milk. We had leased it for a year so we had to do the best we could with it. The second floor was all in one room. We boarded off part of it with rough boards, pasted paper over the cracks, and fixed it for a living place. During the cold weather (and 1882–3 was a cold winter, going as low as 64 degrees below) when the fire in the stove went out, the strips of paper would contract and break with a noise like a pistol shot. After a long time poor Mulholland arrived with our goods. He was a very dilapidated-looking object. He had suffered from snow blindness and had a veil of green netting over his eyes. His face was black in spots from frost bites and his fingers badly frozen.

We lost no time in opening out our goods ready for business. What a time we did have. Many days would pass without a customer. It was depressing. How we did regret our adventure, our goods away down the river, doing nothing, and the provisions we brought in overland soon sold out with no way to get any more till spring. We made one very fortunate sale toward the end of the winter. In our car we had brought a quantity of coal oil in tins. An outfit with sleighs from Battleford came in to get supplies as everything was sold out there, including oil. They offered us two dollars a gallon for what oil we had left, which we promptly accepted. Afterwards we learned that this party encountered stormy weather going back and had to lighten their loads by making a cache in a bluff. Later someone came on it and raided the cache, carrying off the coal oil.

During the winter my partner and I cooked our own food—batching is the expression. The worst part of the cooking was washing up the dishes. We got onto a scheme of using up all our crockery and utensils till all we possessed was dirty. Then we had a great general wash up, one washing and the other drying. The first time I ventured to cook rice was a great event. I put the rice in a milk pan on top of the stove with water enough to cover the rice. Gradually the blooming stuff swelled and swelled and better swelled, I taking out rice to avoid overflowing and continued ladling it out till I had out nearly all that I had put in. Even then it was too thick. We were able to buy bread which was a comfort. The bread we cut in slices as it got so cold in our house that the loaf froze so hard that it was impossible to cut. We toasted the slices to thaw them out. In our innocence we bought some cordwood that was green! It was a terrible job getting it to burn. It was my duty to saw this wood then split it into fine pieces. Oh! the starting of the fire in the morning was a delight! The cold numbed your fingers even with mitts on. This wet stuff simply refused to take fire and sometimes it was half an hour before the fire was going well.

The arrival of the mail stage was the only break in the monotony of existence. It made a trip once every three weeks. The looking forward to its arrival and hoping to have a budget of correspondence buoyed up our spirits. Then the keen disappointment when the expected letters did not arrive depressed us near to heartbreaking. But hope springs eternal in the human breast and we began to look forward to the next stage.

During the winter of 1882–3 there was considerable restlessness amongst the Half-breeds in the settlements around Prince Albert. Meetings were being held frequently and in the discussions a number of white men were taking part in sympathy with the grievance of the Half-breeds. One man particularly was prominent, William Henry Jackson [or Honoré J. Jaxon] by name. He circulated a lot of pamphlets exciting the Half-breeds to open rebellion against the government. After the Rebellion he was tried at Regina for the part he took in it on a charge of treason-felony but was acquitted on the plea of insanity.

In our store there was not much business doing during these days and there were frequent discussions as to the cause of the excitement. As near as I could understand the matter, the Half-breeds had good grounds for grievance which the government was entirely ignoring.[4] In 1870 the Dominion Government settled with the Manitoba Half-breeds for their title to the lands purchased by the Hudson's Bay Company, giving them scrip to extinguish their Indian title to the land arising from their parentage. There were numbers of Half-breeds outside of Manitoba who had not been settled with. These people had been making their living as hunters, trappers, and freighters and, owing to the country beginning to get settled by the incoming of white people, the buffalo and other game had become scarce. Then there was not enough freighting business to employ them all and consequently it had became impossible for them to get enough food to keep them alive. Another grievance consisted of dissatisfaction in regard to the survey of lands along the river. Numbers of them had located on farms laid out in the old style of ten chains frontage on the river running back two miles, had built their log houses on the banks, and laid out their little fields back from the river. The Dominion Government land surveyors, when they came along, laid out the land on the new system of forty chains square

---

4. Clinkskill identifies these grievances or demands as being: (1) division of the North-West Territories into provinces; (2) granting the Métis of the North-West Territories [Saskatchewan] those privileges conceded to the Métis of Manitoba; (3) that persons already located be secured in title to their holdings; (4) the sale of 500,000 acres of government land, the proceeds of which to be devoted to the establishment of schools, hospitals, and other institutions for the Métis, together with a grant of seed and agricultural implements to the poorer of their number; (5) the reservation of 100 townships of land to be distributed in time to the children of the Métis; (6) a grant of at least $1,000,000 for the establishment of an academy at each Métis settlement; and (7) the improvement of the conditions of the Indian nations.

to the quarter-section. Consequently there was confusion as a man's house would be on one quarter-section and his fields on another. Petitions innumerable were forwarded to the government through various channels. Unfortunately these petitions were pigeonholed or answered without due consideration. Finally the Half-breeds sent for Louis Riel to aid them in their cause and the Rebellion of 1885 ensued.

Cold as the weather was we enjoyed splendid health; certainly in our habitation we had plenty of fresh air. In March the snow began to melt so that in a week or so we could see the bare ground once again. With the near advent of spring our spirits began to rise as we looked forward to the arrival of the steamer with our goods. The 20th April saw the ice go out of the river. It was a grand sight. The river at Prince Albert was half a mile wide. The snow having melted quickly, the ice had risen by the pressure of the water. The ice was firm, not much honeycombed, and came down in immense masses, acres in extent—clear, greeny looking masses crashing on the banks and piled up thirty feet high in some places.

Old residents told us that just as soon as the river was clear of ice the steamer would start up the river. Day after day we watched for its arrival. At last one afternoon, about the 20th May, we heard the whistle. Lo and behold, here it was at last. It was a strange-looking craft to my eyes: about a hundred and fifty feet long by fifty feet wide with a large upper structure where the passenger cabins and dining room were and the paddle wheel at the stem. The freight was on deck, there being only a small hold as it was flat bottomed and very shallow. We lost no time in presenting our bills of lading and were informed that all freight and storage charges at Cumberland House, during the nine months it was on the way, had to be paid before we got delivery of a piece. The freight charges we expected we had to pay but the storage charges were an imposition; it was adding insult to injury. We paid it under protest and took delivery. Afterwards we got this charge refunded. In the meantime we consulted a lawyer who gave us an opinion of the law but, as he did not have his law books at hand, advised us not to act on his advice. There was a charge—$25—all the same.

Now we were confronted with the problem of what to do with our goods. Here we were with a large stock of goods bought for the winter trade and this was the month of May. It was rumored that at Battleford, one hundred and fifty miles up the river, there was a shortage of supplies. This place was the capital of the North-West Territories at that time. A troop of the North-West Mounted Police and the residences of the Lieutenant-Governor and the Stipendiary Magistrate, the only judge in the country, were all located there. After debating the matter I decided to go up on the steamer, taking a small assortment of goods with me, to look over the situation.

I arrived at Battleford on the 25th May 1883. The only place I could find in which to put my goods was a log house on the flat on the Battle River below the Government House. The house had been abandoned on account of a flood the spring before. The owner, P.G. Laurie, owner of the *Saskatchewan Herald*, put it at my disposal. It was evident to me that there was an opening for us. I received great encouragement from many of the people to establish a permanent business there. I went back to Prince Albert on the steamer, packed up a larger assortment of goods and, on the next trip of the steamer up the river, again went to Battleford. I brought with me a large tent which I erected on the flat and opened for business. For a few months business was good and the prospect favorable of eventually getting a full share of the trade. It became necessary to arrange for a building as I could not continue in a tent when the cold weather arrived. There was a small log building unoccupied, near the foot of the hill coming in from the south, which had been used as a trading post. Hunting up the owner, I purchased it. In September I made a trip to Prince Albert to get some flour and talk over future movements with my partner. We decided to abandon Prince Albert and locate permanently in Battleford. In October my partner, having sold the bulk of the stock, packed up what was left and came up the trail with the outfit.

Shortly before this I had made a trip to Winnipeg via Swift Current and obtained a further supply of goods. I made the trip to the railway in a buckboard. Coming home the passenger train only ran as far as Regina where I stayed overnight. I had to sleep in a tent, there being no proper hotel accommodation. I got on a construction train in the morning bound for Swift Current. We found difficulty arranging for the freighting of our stock from the railway. The freighters in the business, who had been employed by the other stores, would not work for us. I managed to engage enough carts belonging to some Half-breeds who did not live at Battleford. The trail was poor; it had just been located that summer, was difficult to follow, and was very lumpy. In traveling, the load swayed from side to side as the wheels went over the lumps.

In January I made a trip to Prince Albert to get some flour. I traveled with a Half-breed using a number of jumpers (small sleighs made entirely of wood and drawn by a single pony) to bring back the flour. The weather was intensely cold and every now and then I had to get out and run to keep myself from freezing. We took the north trail, crossing the Saskatchewan at the fork of the Battle River, then straight across country, crossing the river again at Carlton, then along through the pine woods to Prince Albert. One night we camped with some Indians who were on a hunt, trapping fur animals. I camped in their tepee. Never again was I persuaded to camp in a tepee. It is a conical tent with a hole at the apex. A fire is built in the center, the smoke going out at the top. You cannot stand upright or you will be choked with smoke; you have to crouch or lie down all the time. When you go to bed, one side is fiercely warm from the fire; the other side is freezing cold on account of draught of air, the curtain being kept raised to let in air to make the fire burn. It being a case of rolling from one side to the other all night, sleep was out of the question. On the return journey we got to within eighteen miles of Battleford about dark. After eating supper we decided to make for home that night, I being afraid to stay all night as the cold was so intense. When the moon rose we started off; it was still and a slight haze or "haur," as a Scot would say, filled the air. Getting near the river my pony stopped suddenly, refusing to go on. I alighted and went forward to see what was the matter. The poor beast had stopped right on the edge of a cut bank, the frozen river being forty or fifty feet below. I got a scare. Retracing my way I found the right trail leading down to the river. As I ran alongside the jumper, the icicles which had formed on my moustache tinkled like sleigh bells. About two o'clock in the morning I arrived home thankful to be in shelter once again.

In February a "bachelors' ball" was held, my introduction to this kind of thing as held in the North-West. It was a great event. A log storehouse belonging to the largest store was the dancing room. It had a rough floor of spruce boards just as they came from the saw. The light was from coal oil lamps in sconces around the walls. Refreshments were served in a tent pitched alongside. In this tent two stoves were kept briskly going to keep the grub from getting frozen. The guests began arriving about seven in the evening and they came from all around, some traveling thirty miles. Everybody was invited. After a ration of tea and fixings, dancing commenced. The dances were strange to me: quadrilles, four- and eight-hand reels, and Red River jigs galore. In the square dances the master of ceremonies called off the figures: salute your partners, all hands round, chassey all, and grand chain all the way round, were some of the calls. The Red River Jig was a *pièce de résistance*. A couple got up and danced fancy steps opposite one another; then another lady would get up, cutting out the one on the floor; next a man would get up and cut out the man dancing. This went on interminably. The musician, a Half-breed fiddler, got fairly excited. Enthused with the spirit of the dancers he fiddled and fiddled, his feet beating time, legs and whole body in motion, his long black hair waving, and the perspiration rolling off his face. It was a great sight! Everyone so thoroughly enjoyed the dancing that one felt pleased to see the wholehearted way they threw themselves into the enjoyment of the performance. The scene was picturesque. Many of the men were members of the Mounted Police in their red coats. The girls were dressed in the greatest variety of colors: bright green, pink, brilliant red, and canary colored dresses all blending in the color scheme. The matrons, of course, had their babies along. These, wrapped in moss bags, occasionally called for attention, the rest of the time sleeping peacefully while packed away in a corner or hung on a nail stuck in the wall. The dancing kept up till along about nine the next morning. After eating breakfast sleighs were brought around, horses hitched, and, singing gaily, the company departed for home. This was my first experience of a dance in the North-West. Many a one did I assist at afterwards, but the memory of that occasion will always remain fresh in my recollection.

Early in March 1884 I went to Winnipeg via Duck Lake and Troy on the CPR. It was impossible to travel to Swift Current as the trail had not been used during the winter. The snow was deep and the location of the trail not defined. If we had attempted it the crust on the snow, formed by the daytime sun melting the top and the cold at night making it a cake of ice, would have cut our ponies legs all to pieces. We crossed on to the north side going via Carleton to Duck Lake, then following the stage route by Batoche, Hoodoo, Humboldt, and Touchwood to Troy. We had twelve jumpers, one bobsleigh, and a number of loose ponies. We camped in the open, making camp by shoveling snow away, making a bank all around, building a fire in the center, placing a few boughs on the ground, spreading our robes on these making a bed, and sleeping with our feet to the fire. The weather being very cold, it was roughing it for sure. I was glad to get to the railway. It took us ten days to make the trip. One of my men and I went to Regina to get a permit to import liquor to Battleford for our own use. In those days no liquor could be taken into the Territories unless accompanied by a permit issued by the Lieutenant-Governor. Regina had made great strides since my last visit. Houses were built all over and we stayed at a comfortable hotel, the Palmer House, run by an American. After visiting A.E. Forget, clerk to the Lieutenant-Governor, we got what we wanted and took the train to Winnipeg.

On the 3rd April 1884 I got married in Winnipeg and early in May started for Battleford with my wife. At Swift Current we found our transport ready. It consisted of a buckboard, in which my wife and I rode, and a wagon and team of horses to carry our baggage and provisions. By this time I was sufficiently versed in handling a pony to be trusted to drive. The trail was rough as there had not been enough traffic to wear down the hillocks which abounded in that region. These hillocks made the rig sway like a ship rolling and my wife became seasick from the motion. The first day's journey brought us to the crossing of the South Branch, 30 miles from Swift Current. The valley here reminded me very much of the Qu'Appelle valley, very picturesque with a long slope on the south side leading down to a flat and the banks on the other side sloping gradually up from the river. A farmer and his wife going to Battleford to settle traveled along with us for a while. They had some cows with them and, as long as we kept together, we got a supply of fine milk. We soon left them, however, as they could only go slowly on account of the cattle.

We experienced great difficulty locating water, sometimes having to travel long hours before we could camp. On the third day we got into rolling land which continued to Eagle Creek, about halfway. After this we were more fortunate in striking water at lesser intervals. It was my wife's first experience of travel on the prairie and she took it all in good part, not complaining but longing to get to our destination. The ninth day out we made an Indian reserve 13 miles from Battleford. Here we got into a log house in which the farm instructor, Jim Payne, lived. My wife enjoyed having a roof overhead once more. The following day we arrived at Battleford.

Shortly before this time I had purchased a log house with a thatch roof situated on the hillside overlooking the Battle River, a beautiful location. The house was about 18 by 20 all in one, the ceiling being seven feet high. The second storey was floored with rough boards and the heavy rafters supporting the roof were poplar poles with the bark peeled off, the thatch showing through. When we arrived and my wife saw the palatial mansion (it was one of the best in town at that time, outside of the government buildings) to be her home, she did not say very much but I could see she was thinking a lot. The cases containing our furnishings were ranged around the walls, nothing unpacked. We soon set to work and made comparative comfort of our lot. After we had become accustomed to our surroundings we planned an extension at the back, building on a log addition for a kitchen with a second floor and dividing the downstairs into two apartments by running a partition the long way of the house. It was impossible to employ skilled workmen but some Half-breeds undertook to put up the log walls and an old handyman, John Williscraft, undertook to do the carpenter work. He was slow at his work and it was irritating to watch him whittling away. He pottered along till winter set in and then went off to Frog Lake to work for the Roman Catholic Mission. The work was not completely finished as an opening was left where the roof joined onto the original building. When the winter came the air in the house was about the same as that outside; everything froze up solid in the night. I gave my wife the benefit of my experience while batching and she cut up the bread into slices, thawing them up by toasting when required.

During all the summer and fall of 1884 there were frequent rumors of

Half-breed runners traveling around visiting the different Indian reserves. These men attended the council meetings of the Indians and were, we strongly suspected, inciting the Indians to join the Half-breeds in their cause against the goverment. One influential Battleford Half-breed was strongly suspected of furnishing arms and ammunition to the Indians. He was watched carefully as it was thought that he was caching them in bluffs where the Indians could get them.

In June an incident occurred that gave us a good scare. At Lucky Man's Reserve when the instructor was issuing rations, he was assaulted by an Indian. The officer commanding the Police went out with a small detachment of men to arrest the Indian. When the Force arrived at the reserve a body of Indians were assembled holding a Thirst Dance and, as was usual at such times, they were greatly excited. The Police considered it wise to remove the government cattle and stores to Poundmaker's Reserve. Here the Police raised a breastwork of flour bags and prepared to defend their position should they be attacked. The demand that the prisoner be given up was refused and messengers were dispatched to the barracks for more men. Next day a conference was held between the Police and the chiefs. The latter professed to be willing to give up the prisoner but declared the young men would not consent. Finally Poundmaker, Big Bear, and some other Indians offered to go with the Police to the barracks. When the party was preparing to leave the offending Indian came forward to tell his story of the assault. He was at once arrested and four of the Police who effected it were surrounded and a fracas started. Happily in the mix-up no shot was fired; if that had occurred there would certainly have been bloodshed. The prisoner was secured and taken into Battleford. The incident went far to prove the suspicion that the Indians were being incited to rebel against the whites. When the messengers came into the barracks asking for assistance, the civilians formed a company to assist the Police if necessary. A cordon of watchers was formed all round the town to give the alarm if there should be any concerted action. All night the sentries paced their beats till the next forenoon when the Police arrived with their prisoner.

In the fall of the year the Indian agent going round the reserves paying the Indians their annuities, or "treaty money," found them very saucy and difficult to handle. After each band was paid the members hit the trail for town to spend their wealth. The spending of this money was the occasion for great festivities, holding tea dances and pow-pow amongst themselves. The payments at this time amounted to a larger sum than usual on account of large numbers appearing for the first time since some of the treaties had been made. Consequently there were arrears coming to many of the families. In anticipation of this trade we had provided a good stock of goods peculiar to the wants of the Indians and we corralled the biggest share of the money spent. Before beginning to trade, the Indians held a pow-pow in front of each store; long speeches by the chiefs poured forth and presents were made to the trader. He gave presents in return, a highly colored blanket for the chief, tea, tobacco, and biscuits for all and then, after asking that the goods be sold at "bargain prices," the trade began. Every one of the help had to keep their eyes skinned, the squaws particularly appropriating anything in reach without making the necessary pecuniary arrangement usual in a business transaction.

At night, when sundown came, they flocked off to their camp making the night hideous with the perpetual beating of the tom-tom and monotonous *hi-hi-ing* that accompanied it, which was kept up all night. During the day the town was kept lively as they rode around showing off the multi-colored blankets they had purchased. Some of the ponies had young ones on their backs, the number on each pony only being limited by the length of the animal from neck to crupper. After the trading was finished the agent, failing to persuade them to go back home to the reserves, had to call on the Police who drove them out. The Stonies on arriving home had a great lamentation; a prairie fire had run through the reserve burning their dead which they did not bury but placed in trees. The agent informed them it was punishment for staying in town so long!

In the month of August a visit was made to Battleford by the Rev. James Robertson (Lang Jamie, as he was called colloquially), superintendent of the Presbyterian Home Missions, to establish a Presbyterian Mission. As there was no hall available I got permission to use an old log house on the flat that had been abandoned, fixing it with boards on top of soap boxes to serve as pews. The congregation was limited in numbers but earnest. My risibility was aroused watching the preacher, who was a tall man, trying to avoid the rough poles forming joists for the upper floor as he got enthused in his address and moved around. Shortly after there was a small log building erected halfway between the rivers, with services being held regularly. In 1885 this building was moved uptown and in 1886 a nice brick church was built.

Toward the end of November 1884 I made a trip to Winnipeg via Swift Current to buy a stock of Christmas goods. A Half-breed, Jim Bird, accompanied me. Our outfit consisted of one bobsleigh and ten jumpers. On the way back with our outfit the weather was very cold. Starting from Swift Current with a full load on each sleigh everything went well as far as the river. The ice had just formed and was smooth and slippery; we threw sand on the ice to give the ponies a foothold for their unshod hoofs. After struggling for a whole day we landed our outfit on the other side. Snow was very light, ceasing altogether after a few miles. It was hard pulling the sleighs over the bare ground. The ponds all being frozen to the bottom, there was no water for the poor animals. The best time we could make was about ten miles a day. Getting on the higher level beyond Eagle Creek we found snow in patches which improved matters somewhat. The cold was intense with a brisk wind blowing. On stopping for our midday meal we had to keep our mitts on while eating or our fingers would have frozen. The fifth day out saw the last of the firewood used up so we opened cases and, putting stuff into sacks, used the empty cases for fuel in our little sheet-iron tent stove which we used when camping at night. Noon of the next day we pulled into the woods and you can imagine the fire we built without any delay. It thawed us out for once on the trip and we remained in camp all that day and the next, giving our ponies a chance to rest, eat, and drink all they wanted. When about twenty-five miles out of Battleford our man, Dan Ross, met us with a good fresh team and a bobsleigh. He had been sent out to search for us. Some nicely disposed people had started a rumor that we had lost our way and were badly frozen! We were thankful to see him anyway. His team replaced ours in the bobsleigh and we made better time after that, camping that night at the Stoney Reserve eighteen miles from town. During the night my Half-breed played me a dirty trick. In our load was a keg of brandy for which I had a permit. The brandy belonged to a man in town. The Half-breed purloined this keg and set off by himself before we were up in the morning. We found him at a farm house a little further on having a high old time with the contents of the keg. Seeing our brigade coming over the hill, he made off across country for his own home in the Eagle Hills. I rescued what was left of the liquor, arriving home in the afternoon. I was very wrathy over his escapade, especially as the stuff did not belong to me. A luxury of that kind was considered of a value beyond rubies, particularly at Christmas time. However, I cooled down and, taking into account the hard trip we had come through and the consideration he had shown in trying to make me as comfortable as possible, I overlooked his breach of trust. My wife had been very anxious about our long delay in getting home and much distressed by the stories afloat of our having got lost and being frozen.

Rumors were getting more persistent of the disaffection amongst the Half-breeds at Duck Lake and Batoche. Every few days strangers were seen traveling around the reserves. Riel had arrived at Batoche some time in the summer, holding meetings at the Half-breed settlements and fomenting trouble. The impression was that these runners were inciting the Indians to rise as they were becoming more saucy every day. This was confirmed long afterward by the finding of a letter in Poundmaker's camp. It had been written and sent after the fight at Duck Lake and was as follows:

> Praise God for the success He has given us. Capture all the Police you possibly can. Reserve their arms. Take Fort Battleford, but save the provisions, ammunition and arms. Send a detachment of one hundred men.

With a view of defending ourselves, permission was asked of the Minister of Militia to allow us to form a company of militia. In the beginning of March this was done and the unit was called the Battleford Rifles, with Captain E.A. Nash as the commandant. Fortunately there was an ample supply of rifles (of a kind) with an abundance of ammunition in the barracks to arm the men and also the Home Guards which was organized some time afterwards. It is not my intention to go into the whole history of the Rebellion as I have not access to the necessary documents. I intend to restrict my narrative to events of which I was personally cognizant.

Chapter Two:
Insurrection, April to August 1885

A NYONE TRAVELLING OVER THE PRAIRIE between the two Saskatchewan Rivers and seeing the numerous homesteads and the immense fields of grain is struck by the marked contrast to the conditions existing in 1885. Then the prairie was one vast expanse without any people, except here and there such small settlements as Saskatoon, Batoche, or Bresaylor outside of the towns of Prince Albert and Battleford. The old traders' trails worn into many ruts from the passage of the Red River carts were the routes of travel. The long brigades of these carts with their wooden wheels and wooden axles devoid of any grease—musical in the extreme—had worn these ruts deep into the soil. There were no signs of road allowances and the trails had been made to allow of the easiest progression in the general direction of travel. Now and again the stages for Prince Albert, Battleford, and Edmonton carrying Her Majesty's mail were to be met. Apart from these evidences of man's occupation there was nothing else to indicate the presence of civilization. Now there is an entire change of scene; farmhouses, barns, and cultivated fields are to be seen all over the landscape. The advent of the iron road has done away with the use of old trails which are now almost obliterated, except in small sections here and there. In these former days during the time of the "trouble," as it was called, we had to travel warily from bluff to bluff in fear of being way-laid by some hostile Indians or Half-breeds. During the troublous time and for a year afterwards was the only occasion on which

I found it necessary to carry firearms, having a 32-revolver in a holster in my belt. Fortunately I never had to use it.

At this time the Battleford village consisted of a few scattered dwellings. The government buildings—consisting of Government House (recently vacated by the Lieutenant-Governor), the residences of the Judge [Stipendiary Magistrate], Registrar, Indian Agent, and Indian Department office—were built on the brow of the hill on the south of the Battle River. There were a few other dwellings on the slope leading down to the River, those of the Hudson's Bay factor and my own amongst them. On the south side of the North Saskatchewan and between it and the Battle River on an elevated plateau were the North-West Mounted Police barracks, the Hudson's Bay store, A. Macdonald's store, the Roman Catholic Mission, a new building we [Mahaffy-Clinkskill] had just had erected for a store, and about twenty dwellings.

The Police barracks consisted of the Commanding Officer's house, several barracks rooms, storehouses, and stables. These were surrounded by a stockade built of logs set on end about eight feet high, making an enclosure about two hundred yards each way. There were two gates in the stockade, one on the north side and another on the south side. Attempts had been made to build bastions at each corner but they were not of much use as bastions. A new log building had just been erected outside the square on the west side for a barracks room. It was not quite finished and was used by the Battleford Rifles, a local volunteer corps, during the siege. The quartermaster's store was also outside the square.

During the week 22nd to 29th March a large draft from the Police force at Battleford had been sent to Carlton to reinforce Superintendent Crozier's command there, only a few men for routine and those in hospital being left in the barracks. We had been hearing rumours of impending trouble for some days. A number of those residents on the south of the Battle River held a meeting in the house of the Registrar, W.J. Scott. Amongst those present were Judge Rouleau, his brother Dr. Rouleau, Mr. Berthiaume, Inspector of Public Works, Indian Agent J.M. Rae, Hudson's Bay Factor William McKay and myself. We arranged then that should any rising take place we would all assemble in the judge's house and defend it till relieved. This arrangement was not carried out.

On Friday night, 27th March, we got word of the fight at Duck Lake. We began to fear that we were in for trouble. Many whispered conferences were held amongst the white people and friendly Half-breeds. No definite information could be got from those in authority as to what was transpiring, nor would they give us any advice as to what we should do in the event of the little town being attacked. The next two days were spent in grave anxiety. Early on Sunday afternoon, 29th March I was informed that Judge Rouleau, Agent Rae and others were getting ready to send off their families to Swift Current. A number of us got together and had a talk over the situation in McKay's house. It was decided to despatch a trusty Half-breed to Poundmaker's Reserve to see if there were any signs of excitement amongst the Indians. We knew the dispositions of the chiefs were not so unfriendly towards the Whites but these chiefs had very little control over the band. Should the young men become excited over the news of the defeat of the Police at Carlton (which news they had received in some mysterious way before we did) nothing would restrain them from going to any extreme.

About four o'clock the messenger got back with the news that the Indians were on the road, looting and burning property on their way in. By this time the party for Swift Current had set out and this decided our course. Gathering our clothing, etc., together we hastily took a meal and prepared to take refuge in the Police barracks. All our horses were off on a trip to Swift Current for goods for the spring and all I had was a little pony my wife used to drive and a buckboard. Everyone else owning any teams were using them themselves to take their belongings to a place of safety so I was unable to take any of our trunks. My wife carried her jewel case and an old family Bible, an heirloom, in her hands. These and the clothing on our backs was all we could take. The river was in bad shape for crossing as the bridge, which was always taken down before the ice went out, had been removed. Water was running at each side of the strong ice in the centre. One had to take a boat to cross the water, walk across the ice, and then take another boat to get to the other side. I went down stream with the empty buckboard to cross at a shallow part and in crossing nearly drowned the little pony. When we arrived at the barracks we found that besides the townspeople a number of the settlers had come in with their families. There was an excited knot of people. My wife got accommodation in the Commanding Officer's house in a room with several other women.

The men immediately formed a company of Home Guards and got rifles and ammunition from the Police stores. I was detailed for duty on guard. It was a cold night; sleet and rain were falling as I tramped back and forward on my beat, straining my eyes for any moving object. I could not realize the dangerous state we found ourselves in. The next morning we were horrified to see a large crowd of Indians on the top of the hill where the government buildings were situated. They were marching around in all the glory of paint and feathers. We could see them roaming around peering into the windows of the houses, evidently disappointed to find the inmates had gone.

Early in the forenoon some Half-breeds came over to the barracks as a deputation, asking that the Indian Agent go over to have a conference with the Indians. Poundmaker's message to the agent was that the Indians had heard of a fight between the Police and the Half-breeds and that as soon as the Police had done with them they would turn on the Indians. They only wanted an assurance from the agent that it was not so, together with the gift of some tea and tobacco, and they would return to their reserves. These same "peaceable and well-disposed Indians" had the previous night raided the houses of three settlers on the Battle River, burning some of them, and had driven off a hundred head of choice cattle and fifty horses. This having been done, they wanted to have a friendly chat with the agent! He offered, however, to have a palaver with them should the chiefs come across the Battle River and meet him midway between the barracks and the river. They would then be covered by the rifles of the barracks. This offer was refused. The Hudson's Bay officer, who had remained over night on the south side, strongly advised the agent not to go to their camp. One of the loyal Half-breeds even offered to stake his life on his safety. The Half-breed, whom we had suspected during the winter of supplying arms and ammunition to the Indians, was seen by us in the early morning arranging the camp and showing where the tepees were to be placed. When he came over he was promptly arrested and placed under guard till the arrival of the troops.

In the afternoon we noticed that a huge fire had been built on the ground opposite the building used as an office by the Indian Agent. Round the fire were grouped the headmen of the bands holding a council. We could hear the beat of the tom-tom and the monotonous *hi-hi* of the Indians. Just about dusk there was a great commotion, shouting and firing off of guns. In the failing light we could see them swarming around the houses; the sound of smashing of doors and breaking of windows could be distinctly heard. That night I was on sentry duty over the magazine and I could see from where I was walking up and down the light of the lanterns they were carrying as they passed in and out of the houses, my own house particularly engaging my attention. That night they raided the Hudson's Bay store, our store, and the private houses. The desolation wrought was only equalled by a fire of whose work we say that "there was nothing saved." The devilish ingenuity displayed in destroying things that were of no use to them would put to the blush of a city mob—a thing supposed to be the extreme of everything that is mad and unreasoning. They had a high time generally, as we found out later.

All day long settlers had been arriving from outside points, bringing with them what little stuff they could snatch in their haste. The question was, where were all these people to be lodged? The women and children were put in the barrack rooms and the Commanding Officer's house. The men had to hustle for themselves; some got into the Indian Department warehouse which was inside the stockade. My poor wife was in a sad plight. The clothing she had packed in our trunks to bring over she never saw again as this night everything in our home had been carried off. What a mercy we came over that Sunday night. It had been planned by these fiends that our houses were to have been surrounded in the night and a general massacre take place. In the meantime we were thankful that our lives were spared.

The morning after everything seemed quieted down. The Indians had evidently withdrawn to some distance as there were none of them in sight. In the afternoon a few of us went down to the river bank to reconnoiter. We did not attempt to cross the river. We saw two men standing in front of a building that the Hudson's Bay Company had been using as a temporary sale shop, a little way up from the bank. We shouted to them and just as they started to come down towards us some rifle shots were fired in our direction from the underbrush on the other side. This was a signal for a hasty retreat to cover as we were standing in the open on the river bank. Hampered as we were with heavy overcoats, carrying a Snider rifle about four feet long, and a belt around our waists filled with cartridges that had ounce bullets in them, it was a wild scamper. There was a pool of water and half-melted snow which we splashed through. I shall never forget the sight of my companions floundering through the water, breathlessly hastening to get out of range. I must confess I did exert myself, too, in the run but the sight of us all scattering in different directions, each scared he was to be a target for a bloodthirsty Indian, was comical in the extreme. This comical side of the incident was intensified when it was discovered that it was not Indians at all who fired the shots but a couple of Irishmen (one of them an old miner, a regular Fenian, and the other the cook at the Industrial School). They had discharged their rifles in sport to see what effect it would have on us. They succeeded in getting some amusement out of our stampede.

Settling down to make preparations for the defence, a second company of Home Guards was formed. The first, No. 1 Company, was under the command of W.J. Scott, the Registrar. The second, No. 2 Company, was under Robert Wyld, a rancher formerly of the Police force. I was a full-fledged private. The warehouse of the Indian Department was cleared out and given to the Home Guards as their barracks room. The old gag of selecting the softest plank to lie on for the night was slightly altered in this case. The floor consisted of whipsawed logs of all thicknesses with wide spaces between. It was a case of selecting the least uneven planks showing the smallest spaces between as these spaces had the faculty of allowing a draft of cold air to shoot up that seemed to cut your flesh like a knife.

Every now and again some more outlying settlers would drop in with stories of their escape. George Gopsil and Tom Hodson had a narrow shave. The Indians caught them and demanded all they had with them but on Hodson giving them a horse as a peace offering they allowed Gopsil to drive on. Just as the wagon had been emptied of the few things the fugitives had hoped to save, a hunchback devil known as Nez Perce

Jack attempted to tear the shawl from the shoulders of Gopsil's child. Joe Price, who was a short distance behind Gopsil, did not fare so well. He was driving along in a wagon with his wife and four children when the marauders compelled them to get down and drove off leaving them afoot ten miles from town. As if this even was not enough, the same hunchback above referred to attempted to strip Mrs. Price of her dress. Gopsil fortunately saw their plight and drove them into town. We had the satisfaction after a while of knowing that this same hunchback got something that was coming to him. Harry Nash, one of our bravest companions, when on escort with the water cart one day, got a shot at him from across the Battle River. The fiend fell and we never heard tell of him again.

News came in of the fate of Barney Freeman, a Belgian on a farm about five miles out on the trail to the Stoney Reserve. He was brutally murdered in his own yard. On Friday two of our friendly Half-breeds went out and brought in the body which presented a horrible appearance and gave evidence of the depth of fiendishness that marked his murder. Not satisfied with shooting him twice from behind while he was engaged in greasing his wagon, the fiends inflicted two frightful gashes on his head just above his right ear. They also fired a bullet through his head hours after he was dead, the gun being held so close as to burn the skin, and fired an iron-shod arrow into his breast as he lay stretched in death. He died with the wagon wrench in his hand, showing how he had been employed when the fatal shot was fired. He usually carried a watch but nothing of value was found on the body when searched. The house was completely gutted and the little that was not carried away being scattered around in utter wantonness.

Poor Barney, I knew him well. He was a bachelor who often called in at my house on his way home from town and had a chat with my wife and I. He took great enjoyment out of my wife's cooking. Barney had led a roving life and had been some time in the western States. His brother having been killed by Indians there, he had a great hatred of all Indians. He never would let them on his place, driving them off whenever any of them would come near. He came up to the West working on the construction of the government telegraph line, before leaving the service and taking up a farm with Tom Dewan as partner.

On Wednesday the first of April some of the settlers from the Bresaylor settlement came in with their families. These consisted of the Scotch Half-breeds in this settlement. The others, the French Half-breeds, did not come in with them. At midnight one of the French Half-breeds came in saying the settlement was in danger and asked for an escort to bring in the people and their cattle. He came in such haste as to startle the sentries; an alarm was given and every man turned out to defend our position. Colonel Morris, however, did not have faith in his stories, which were contradictory, so he caused him to be put in the lock-up. It came out afterwards that his coming was a ruse to try to get a small party of our men in such a position as to be ambushed.

The situation inside the barracks was getting acute. There were about one hundred able-bodied men with about three hundred women and children. The difficulty was to get shelter for them and food for so many. A number of the women and children were housed in the quartermaster's warehouse outside the stockade. In the night time frequent alarms were sounded and every man took his appointed station at a loophole made in the stockade. When these alarms were given the women and children had to clamber over the barrier to get inside, some of the women in their excitement throwing the children over. This could not continue. A large marquee [canopy] in the Police stores was rooted out and erected in the square where these people were made as comfortable as possible. I got hold of some canvas and had a tent eight feet by ten made in which my wife and I slept. My wife could not endure the closeness of the house in which there were about sixty women and children. I fixed up a kind of bed for my wife and those nights when I was not on guard duty I slept on the ground with all my clothes on, the cartridge belt around my waist and my loaded rifle by my side.

The question of food was a serious matter. A party of skirmishers was sent over to see what was left in the stores. They reported some flour, bacon, and tea could be got. Fortunately our store had received a full carload of flour from Swift Current a short time before. A temporary crossing was constructed and a party with wagons under a strong escort brought over a generous supply of flour, bacon, tea, some tobacco, dried apples, and a very few canned goods. These supplies were piled up in the centre of the square, covered with a tarpaulin, and a strong guard put over it. We began to feel better at the sight of enough food to do us for a time. The flour was all right but oh! that bacon. It displayed all the colours of the rainbow and tasted rank. However, it was edible if you had a strong appetite and a vigorous digestion. There was no well in the barracks so all the water was obtained from the Battle River, a distance of over a mile, and had to be drawn in tanks with a regular escort accompanying the wagons. The danger of the supply being cut off was always present and we should have been in a sad plight if such should have occurred.

Now that we had settled down into some sort of shape inside the barracks, we began to think of our friends who were not with us. The instructor on the Grizzly Bear's Head Reserve, James Payne, had not turned up. On the morning of Tuesday, before starting to join Poundmaker's band, the Stonies began their fiendish work by murdering Payne. His body was found on a manure heap by the relief column when it reached the reserve. The head was fearfully bashed in. On the trail from Swift Current at the time of the outbreak were Frank Smart, Dan Ross, Bob MacDonald, and others freighting in supplies for the stores. We knew they would have to come right through the Indian reserves in the Eagle Hills. They got in on the 13th April, having cached the carts and goods off the trail. MacDonald, who had left his goods near the South Saskatchewan River, had gone back to Swift Current. On his way back when he got to the cache he found that it had been rifled, the loads had been broken open, and what was not carried away scattered around on the prairie. No news had come to us about the people at Fort Pitt and Frog Lake. These were in the midst of the Indian reserves and should there be a rising amongst them the white people would be in great danger as they would be helpless against so many.

To come back to the doings of the earlier days of our siege: some adventurous spirits broke barracks one night and crossed the Battle River to see the condition of the deserted houses over there. In going through the Industrial School building (formerly the Lieutenant-Governor's residence) it was found that nearly everything portable had been carried off. The stuff that could not be carried away was destroyed and the fragments scattered all around. Visiting Judge Rouleau's house, in which a room had been used by his brother Dr. Rouleau, as a dispensary, the medicines were found untouched; the idea being that the fear of getting poisoned caused them to leave them severely alone. Here the boys made a great find, no less than a quantity of good spirits which the Indians had over-looked, possibly thinking it was nauseous medicine or poison. These lads soon tested the liquor and came back to barracks showing evidence of its potency. They were severely reprimanded by the Officer Commanding and warned of the consequence of again leaving without permission.

On Thursday, 3rd April, ten of us got leave to go over the Battle River and view the damage. After getting across the river we advanced in open order several paces apart with rifles loaded, ready for action. None of the enemy were sighted. We approached the different houses very cautiously, one of the party going in at the doorway and the others standing around covering the windows and doorways with rifles. The sight that met us when we entered my house was pitiful. I shall never forget it. In the hall was a large round-topped trunk that had contained a lot of my wife's clothing. The top had been smashed in, no attempt having been made to force the fastenings. It was entirely empty. In the dining room was the table at which we had taken a hurried meal before fleeing to the barracks and all the dishes, etc., had been left on it. Evidently the Indians had eaten what food had been left by us and then taken a club and smashed the dishes. On the table I found a large plug of tobacco with a little piece cut off the corner, about enough to fill a pipe. From the china closet many of the dishes had been carried off. All the tea cups were gone but the saucers, which no Indian uses, were left behind, as were a number of plates. The cupboard where the silver was kept was quite empty and all the fine silver and cutlery my wife had received as marriage presents was gone.

In the bedrooms nothing was left that could be easily carried. The bedsteads and mattresses were there but all blankets, sheets, pillows, etc., were gone. The mirrors in the bureaus were all broken and the trunks, drawers, etc., were empty. A fine writing desk had been broken open and the contents scattered on the floor. The books (I had a good library) had been taken from the shelves, torn apart, and the leaves scattered around.

It was a distressing sight, especially when it is borne in mind that we had been married only a year, that my wife's mother and my mother had died after our marriage, and, we being in mourning, my wife had not worn any of her wedding trousseau. To know that all the dresses and numerous valuable wedding presents, all her extensive stock of napery, etc., were gone, made one pause and vow vengeance on the hideous brutes that had robbed us.

Roaming around the cellar I found a treasure trove—half a dozen fresh eggs. Just fancy what that meant, considering the nature of our rations of green bacon. There was also a bottle containing about three fingers of square face gin. This was evenly divided amongst us. The eggs we kept for a mother who had had a baby just after getting into the barracks. In the garden I found a clock and a fine work box of inlaid ivory and ebony ready for removal. The box was an heirloom brought from China by my wife's uncle. The box was broken open, the glass mirror in the lid broken, and the little carved ivory spindles, bobbins, and tatting needles broken. It was evidence of the malicious devilment of the savage. The Indian Department office was the next building we visited. The files had been taken out of the frames and the papers torn and scattered about. Everything that could be imagined in the way of destruction had been carried out.

In the store the shelves were emptied of goods, the bins containing groceries were empty, the weighing scales smashed, and the counters hacked, evidently by axes. On the second floor the shelving along one wall had been filled with some thousands of cigars. The boxes had been swept off the shelves and then trampled on, the fragments of cigars mixed with pieces of the boxes and torn paper. Fortunately my partner had carried our valuable papers, records, and books to the barracks with him. The little iron safe was the only thing that resisted their efforts of destruction. There had been in an adjoining storehouse a number of bales of furs all packed for shipment. The ropes binding the furs had been cut and the valuable furs put into sacks that had contained oats with the oats emptied out knee deep on the floor and the less valuable skins mixed up with them. This was my last visit to the store. Two nights later the building was set on fire and completely destroyed, the only thing left to indicate a building had been there being a hole in the ground where the cellar had been.

It was suspected that a camp of Half-breeds existed near the town. A detachment of twelve men was sent out with a guide and the camp was found about two miles out in a ravine. On seeing us they threw up their hands. They were gathered in and the outfit of horses, carts, wagons, and buckboards were confiscated. Six of the men were put in the lockup and their families made to camp near the barracks outside the stockade. The other five men were released on parole as they were able to give a satisfactory explanation of their presence in the camp.

On the afternoon of Thursday a man named Wright came down on the north side of the Saskatchewan from Turtle River. He reported having met Moosomin's and some of Thunderchild's band on the north side. They assured him of their loyalty. They had plundered the instructor's house and were killing government cattle but considered that as nothing serious, only looking on bloodshed as being wicked.

We had been informed that Colonel Herchmer with a force of Police was on the way from Swift Current. We were anxiously looking out for the party and would have sent some men to meet him but we could not spare any men. The number of our force was so small that it was not adequate to protect the barracks containing so many helpless women and children. The authorities were very reticent regarding outside operations; all we were told was that help was coming, without any particulars. Telegraph communication was intermittent and when it was in operation the line was wholly taken up with government business. Every now and again the line was cut and the repairers displayed great bravery, never hesitating to go out from either the Humboldt end or from Battleford to make good the damage. The line west to Edmonton was altogether out of commission.

Saturday, 4th April, was a gloomy day in our community. A letter from W.J. McLean, the Hudson's Bay factor at Fort Pitt, was received. It gave an account of the terrible massacre at Frog Lake, thirty-five miles west of Fort Pitt, which had been perpetrated on the 2nd of April. The letter was brought in by Henry Quinn, a nephew of one of the murdered men. His account of it is as follows:

A part of Big Bear's band was camped there and pretending to wish for a conference with Mr. Thomas Quinn, acting Indian Agent, invited him to visit them. Thinking it might have something to do with their promised removal to a Reserve, he consented. On his way to the meeting [he] called on Father Fafard and invited him to go along. John Williscraft, a white man working at the Mission, also accompanied them out of curiosity. They had scarcely reached the camp when one of Big Bear's leading men remind[ed] Quinn that he had long ago promised to shoot him, adding that the time had now come. Before they could realize the situation, Williscraft, Quinn, and Father Fafard were killed by successive shots. In the meantime other parties of Indians had been stationed at the houses of the few white men in the vicinity, taking as their signal the firing in the camp. Almost the entire population of the place was simultaneously killed before they had time to realize that they were in danger. The victims of the massacre were: T.T. Quinn, Acting Indian Agent; John Williscraft, carpenter working at the Roman Catholic Mission; John C. Gowanlock, erecting a grist and saw mill; John Delaney, Farm Instructor at Frog Lake; Charles Govin, carpenter working for the Indian Department; Wm. C. Gilchrist, working for Gowanlock; Rev. Father Fafard, Roman Catholic Priest; Rev. Father Marchand, Roman Catholic Priest; Geo. Dill, trader for Mahaffy-Clinkskill. (Mrs. Gowanlock and Mrs. Delaney were reported killed also but we now know they were held as prisoners by Big Bear. John Pritchard and Henry Quinn escaped. Quinn reached Battleford, Pritchard was afterwards captured and held prisoner.)

The heartrending account of the slaying of these people, so well known to us, cast a gloom over our hearts. The men talked in earnest whispers of what they would do if only given a chance at the fiends. Wiser heads realized that the great responsibility of protecting the women and children under our charge prevented any lessening of the force in barracks. It intensified our anxiety regarding the fate of the other white people at Fort Pitt. We got word that the people living at Onion Lake and in the neighbourhood of Fort Pitt had gathered at the Hudson's Bay post. The Police force under Inspector Dickens went into it also, fortifying it by connecting the different buildings with earthen embankments in the hope of being able to hold out till relief should reach them. They had an abundance of arms, ammunition, and supplies. The beleaguered post contained forty people, including the Police.

In the afternoon a large body of mounted Indians was seen on the hill across the Battle River. Sometime afterwards they came near, fired one store and spent the night overhauling the other stores and buildings more with a view to destruction than of looting. We were all on the watch expecting a possible attack on our position. About midnight an alarm was sounded but nothing came of it. During the night, when the store was burning, several rockets were sent up at various points in the Eagle Hills. We imagined these might have been signals given by Police coming to our aid and were inwardly rejoicing. However, we were disappointed; it must have been Indians who set them off. This night I was on guard and from my position I could see the buildings burning. It can easily be imagined with what sorrow I saw my worldly belongings go up in smoke.

Sunday, 5th April, a courier came in from Fort Pitt with further details of the Frog Lake massacre. He brought the report that the Lac la Biche Indians had also risen. Seemingly there was a simultaneous rising among all the tribes. [It would appear that the following passages were taken from Clinkskill's diary as the information is in the present tense.]

> This morning the stables at the Industrial School were set fire to and destroyed. Evidently the savages were drawing out their enjoyment by firing the buildings one at a time. The French settlers at Bresaylor settlement refused to come in, alleging they are safer there than in the barracks but very anxious to know what is going on here. Divine Services were held today by the Presbyterians and Anglicans. There are some splendid brave fellows in our camp. French Canadians, some of them, some loyal Half-breeds and some Scots amongst them, too. The Commanding Officer is never at a loss to get volunteers for despatch carriers. The methods they adopt to conceal their despatches is sometimes amusing. One sewed his on the inside of his moccasins, another under the lining of his cap, and another got his placed under a plaster on his back. The barracks square is now in good shape. The large tent erected for the use of the women and children of

the Taylor settlement is fully occupied. The stockade has been strengthened by boards nailed on the top of the logs. Flour bags have been filled with sand and placed around the inside, one at each loop hole, to protect the man placed there. A ditch is being dug outside the stockade but it is laid out on such a gigantic scale I feel sure will never be finished. Every one takes his turn at fatigue; there is no respect of persons. A minister of the Gospel is gasping at this work alongside a husky young farmer, making the dirt fly.

There were some pitiful cowards amongst us as well as good brave souls. One chap, a French Canadian, was found when an alarm sounded, hiding in a barrel. I was the subject of much merriment one night. As an alarm sounded I was on the way to the guardroom to go on duty. I had a pillow under my arm, to be used when snatching a sleep between my two hours of sentry. I ran for my place at the stockade, carrying my pillow. Those who saw me crouching at my station blamed me for going to have my ease during the expected attack! This sentry outside was no vaudeville stunt, I can assure you. Every little object in the semi-darkness seemed magnified in size. A little bit of a weed seemed to be as large as a man. With your eyes strained, every nerve on edge, mistakes would occur. You had to watch the ground for fear of some Indian crawling up on you. Naturally, the imagination gets working. We were very much bothered by a lot of dogs sneaking around, and pigs too. One night I called "Halt," and challenged. It turned out to be a hog in search of food and the answer I got was a grunt! I think my wife will never let that incident be forgotten. [The following passages are obviously diary entries.]

Monday, 6th April

A courier from Fort Pitt arrived. No news but the Police intend to hold the Fort till not a man is left. We learn that the cattle are being rounded up and taken to Poundmaker's where the grand stand is to be made. Large bodies of Indians are patrolling between the rivers to intercept messengers to and from Pitt. Little Poplar, the wost savage among them, was seen near Pitt with six lodges on his way to join Big Bear.

Tuesday, 7th April

A man appeared on the north side of the Saskatchewan. As he did not respond to signals, a boat went across and found one of our couriers, Joe Poitras. He was snow blind and so could not see our signals. His report is that at Prince Albert there is a good organization waiting for reinforcements. Riel is reported on the south side of the South Saskatchewan, ready for the troops. One of our men, a Half-breed, on his way to Pitt arrived back. He had been captured by some Stonies, robbed of his papers, gun, etc., and set afoot.

Wednesday, 8th April

A number of Indians appeared on the hill near the Industrial School with pack horses. We watched them closely as they called at the different houses. A while afterwards they came back with carts which they started to load up at the Industrial School and other places. Some of them fired on our water carts. The fire was returned, the nine pound cannon being used with shell. A number of our men got behind a pile of cordwood on the brow of the hill looking towards the south. Firing at the Indians as they passed down and up the hill, they sent three or four of them to their happy hunting grounds. After a time, Col. Morris ordered our men back to barracks as he considered it waste of ammunition! None of our men were hurt by the fire of the Indians, though several of their bullets struck the cordwood behind which they were sheltered.

Friday, 10th April

A courier came from Prince Albert and reported that Fort Carlton had been burned. Riel wanted to go to Montana to bring in the soldiers and money he had promised but as his sincerity was doubted, he was not allowed to go. Two of the Half-breeds in his camp, Primeau and Charles Nolin who were in his council, had deserted and gone into Prince Albert, preferring imprisonment to following Riel.

Saturday, 11th April

This is the fourteenth day since we moved into barracks. The anxiety and strain on the nerves is starting to tell on us all. Every one went about his duty with a weary, despondent air. What is being done towards sending us relief. Our thoughts were with our friends at Pitt. Our position was bad enough but we knew they were in much greater danger. The place where the whites had gathered consisted of a few scattered buildings without any stockade around and with heavy timber reaching almost to the buildings. At any time it was possible for an Indian to crawl up and set a fire that would drive all the people into the open. It was astonishing how many of the usual jovial happy souls got to be so irritable under the strain of watching and the fear of attack, the hoping and longing for relief that was promised and never came. From day to day the officials kept saying "Relief is coming, everything is being done to hurry up the Police." We had great faith in the Police boys and we knew well if Col. Herchmer had the matter in his own hands we would long ago have welcomed them into our camp. They did well to tell us the Police were being depended on for our succour. Hugh Richardson, the telegraph operator, was constantly being appealed to tell us what the prospects were. He would not give any information of the movements of the troops. Looking at it now, the reticence seems necessary. In our midst were some Half-breeds whose sympathies we strongly suspected of being with the enemy. Any definite news of the movements of the soldiers under General Middleton would have immediately been conveyed by some mysterious manner to the Indians. On the afternoon of this day Richardson got in touch with the CPR agent at Swift Current and got a dispatch which he could not keep to himself. He posted it outside his office: "Otter's column left this morning." The disappointment of us all was somewhat tempered with the news that some reinforcements had actually left Swift Current. Our hopes had been that Herchmer and his boys had been detailed with this column for our relief. We knew what they could do if they got the opportunity. Still it was comforting to hear that some relief was in sight. New hope was raised in our hearts and everyone went about their work with a cheerful spirit.

Monday, 13th April

The men who had been on the Swift Current trail when the trouble started got in on horseback today: Frank Smart, Dan Ross, Bob MacDonald, Henry Storer, Joe Heon and Jim Bird. They had travelled mostly at night and made a wide detour, travelling across the country and avoiding the beaten trails. From the papers they brought in, excitement in the outside world seemed to be intense over our predicament. The knowledge that troops were on the move gave us encouragement to bear up under the suspense. During this week the smoke of fires was seen in all directions. It was evident that the enemy were constantly on the move as we could see smoke starting in a new place every day. After everything of value had been taken they would end up by setting fire to the buildings.

Monday, 19th April

Events of tragic significance occurred during this and the following few days. At noon two scouts came in from Pitt with the startling and depressing news that the Fort had fallen and all within its protection had been seemingly slaughtered. These men at night reached the river immediately opposite the Fort. There were no lights to be seen in the morning and they could see no one around; the windows and doors were gone. A small camp of Indians was found who told the scouts that the Police had been warned to make their escape which they did by means of a raft on the river. Our fears were that, had the unfortunate victims succeeded in making a raft, it was a splendid opportunity for the savages to pick them off as they floated helpless and exposed on their frail craft. Our anxiety was intensified as time went on and we had no tidings. The party must by this time have been four to five days on the river and the usual time to allow for the trip was two or three days. There had been about fifty white people in all at the Fort as far as we could learn. What had become of the others? The day passed and night came without any tidings. A party of our men had started out soon after we got the news. Their purpose was to scout along the banks of the river, watching for signs of the floating fugitives and to help, if necessary, when found. We could ill spare any of our number but something must be done to relieve the strain of anxiety. On Tuesday evening this party returned, reporting having seen the party about 45 miles off. The next morning the party arrived. They were a weary and travel-stained lot of fellows. They had been five days in an old craft that had been used at Pitt as a ferry-scow. They had a wounded comrade, Constable

C. Loasby, with them. Inspector Dickens, son of the novelist, was in command.

They gave us a full account of the abandonment of the Fort. On Wednesday the 15th, a large body of Indians camped near them and held a council as to the advisability of attacking the Fort. Whilst this was proceeding some crept up near the buildings and fired on the Police picket, killing Const. Cowan and wounding Constable C. Loasby. The Police in the Fort sallied out in support of the picket, driving the Indians back, killing four of them, and wounding several. In the mean time, W.J. MacLean, factor for the Hudson's Bay Company, had gone to the camp to have a parley with the chiefs who made him a prisoner. It was then decided to attack the Fort and massacre all the inmates. He was given the option of bringing all his people into the Indian camp where their lives would be spared, leaving the Police alone, or being himself killed. He sent a letter to his wife explaining the situation. The following is MacLean's letter from Top of the hill, Fort Pitt, dated April 15, 2 p.m.:

My Dear Wife—

Most unfortunately I have been too confiding in the Indians and came into camp. After I had a long talk with them and they had spoken at length with me they would not have it any other way than that the Police should and must go away at once. I was speaking with a view of at the same time gaining time for the three men that are gone. They, the scouts, came on the main road and met some young fellows who fired on them, or they fired on the scouts, and the whole camp was after them in a minute. I thought the Indians were aware of the three men who were out and said nothing about them. Had I spoken perhaps things would have been different. They now, in the excitement, had made me a prisoner and made me swear by Almighty God that I would stay with them.

Alas, that I came into the camp at all, for God only knows how things will go now. They want you and the children to come into camp and it may be for the best that you should for heaven only knows how this will end. If the Police force in the fort cannot get off, the Indians are sure to

attack it tonight—so they say—and will burn it down. I
am really at a loss what to suggest for the best. For the
time being we might be safe with the Indians, but hereafter
it is hard to say for provisions will be scarce after a short
time; we may suffer that way. The Chief and councillors
say they will let me go down the Beaver River with my
friends and if so we will be all right. Stanley must come too
and everyone belonging to the Company. They say
Malcolm and Hodson also are wanted. I will write you
again after I hear what Mr. Dickens says about allowing
you all to come out. I believe candidly it is best you should
come, as the Indians are determined to burn the fort if the
Police do not leave. They have brought coal oil with them
for that purpose and I fear they will succeed in setting the
place on fire. Beyond a doubt the Indians promise that
after you all come out they will go off and give the Police
time to get away before they come to see the fort again.
The Indians wish you to bring all your things at once. We
must do all we can to get out before dark and move out so
as to give Captain Dickens a chance to get off with his
men. They tell me to bring everything I can with me. May
God bless and guide you all for the best.

W.J. MacLean

(The remainder of this letter is personal and private
matter.)

The decision was made at once on receiving this letter. All the people in the Fort, except the Police, commenced preparation to join
MacLean in the camp. The Police, being now from lack of members
unable any longer to defend the Fort, at once prepared to evacuate.
Provisions and ammunition were hurriedly got together, placed in the
scow, and, with their wounded comrade Loasby in their midst, marched
down to the river's edge. The scow was almost full of water and it took
some time to get the water out. This delay was a dreadful suspense,
everyone expecting an attack from the Indians before the boat could get
away. However, at last the party got away and reached the other side of
the river. The weather was cold and stormy and the ice was running,
which made if difficult to make progress. On Tuesday our scouts were
sighted and on Wednesday Battleford was reached.

Monday the 20th was a melancholy, sad night for us all. There was a mounted patrol which rode out around for a few miles every night. The men were selected from Police and civilians, the very best men being detailed. On this occasion six men had gone out riding two and two together in different directions. Frank Smart and Const. White went riding together in a southwesterly direction toward the Battle River. Past the farm of Bill Turner was some little brush and as they passed shots were fired. One of the bullets struck Smart in the middle of the back, coming out just below the nostril with death being instantaneous. The horse bounded forward (it also had been struck) carrying the body some distance before it fell off. White came up and spoke to Smart but on getting no response he immediately galloped back to barracks to report. A strong detachment of the Battleford Rifles sallied out and brought the body in. Poor Smart was a fine, bright, promising, young fellow. He had just run the gauntlet from Swift Current through the Indian country only to be struck down in such a cowardly manner. We were roused to vengeance for the dastardly outrage. Smart, one of our [Mahaffy-Clinkskill] employees in the store, had been married a little over a year, leaving a widow and little baby boy. The next day his remains were buried with military honours in a cemetery on the river bank a few hundred yards from the barracks. Every man in our camp except sentries on guard accompanied the cortege.

Just as we were returning from the grave, a horseman was seen coming down the hill leading to the crossing on the Battle River waving his arms in an endeavour to draw our attention. On some of our men going out to meet him, the horseman proved to be Charlie Ross, one of our old-time members of the Police. He was also an advance scout from Herchmer's force and informed us a relieving force was only a few miles away. It is impossible for me to describe the joy with which this news was received. Women were crying and embracing each other; men went about with a brisk jaunty air; and every eye was brightened as the long suspense was broken at last. We realized our safety was assured. Meantime, the Commanding Officer marshalled the entire force and warned us that this night it was possible the Indians might attack as it was the last chance for them to assault our weak position. I can well remember how every man seemed to clench his teeth and grasp his rifle with a more determined vigour. Scarcely one in the barracks slept a wink that night. When last post was sounded by our bugler, Paddy Burke, we heard an answer faintly in the distance. It was the call from the troops about three miles out, the sweetest music that had ever reached our ears.

About sundown the building on the flat used by the Hudson's Bay Company was set on fire. We could see it with the Indians dancing around in fiendish glee. Suddenly a great flame rose in the air and shortly after a noise like a sharp peal of thunder rent the air and we could feel the tremor of the earth. The building had blown up, whether from gunpowder or coal oil stored in the cellar we can never know. Afterwards we learned that a number of savages who were around the building enjoying the destruction were "accounted for." The house on the hill where Judge Rouleau resided was also burned. There had been a quantity of lumber piled in a shed near the house which it was intended to use in some proposed alteration. This was fired first, then the house. The conflagration made a great display and plainly visible at the camp of the incoming Force. The next morning the troops marched in and camped on the top of the hill. The Force with Colonel Otter in command consisted of The Queen's Own Rifles, Mounted Police, C Company School of Infantry, Ottawa Foot Guards, and a battery of artillery.

After a few days orders were issued that the families within the barracks were to return to their homes! It was known afterwards that Colonel Otter reported "I found the inhabitants unwilling to return to their homes." Well might he report the unwillingness to obey such an order. What irony to address a band of homeless, houseless, penniless people with "go back to your homes." Go back to the scene of desolation without even a change of clothing, without a rooftree over their heads, without a mouthful to eat, and without the wherewithal to purchase food for a meal if food could have been purchased at any price. A few of the citizens in the new town situated close to the barracks, these houses not having been destroyed, went back to their homes. One company of Home Guards moved into town, occupying a large log warehouse belonging to A. MacDonald. This building was loopholed to be ready to resist an attack. I managed to get a small log building of one room about sixteen feet square into which I moved with my wife.

The Queen's Own Rifles were camped on the prairie between the barracks and the town. This seemed to us a most injudicious arrangement. Had we been attacked from the west, in case of an alarm, our women and children would naturally flee to the barracks for protection. The Rifles would be unable to distinguish between friend and foe in the darkness and the fugitives would run the risk of being injured in the consequent excitement and confusion. It used to be said that we the civilians were protecting the Queen's Own instead of them protecting us. Outside the town, west of the houses, were rifle pits which were manned by the Home Guard at night. These pits ran from the Saskatchewan to the Battle River, forming the first line of sentries from darkness to daylight. It was an eerie, lonesome job lying in these pits. One night I was on duty in a pit about halfway across when suddenly I was startled by shots being fired on my extreme right, the bullets striking the earth all around me. It was inexplicable. Had the shots been from the front I could have understood it but coming right along the line of sentries was what puzzled me. Johnny Longmore, in the next pit to me, came running over to see if I could explain matters. We decided to make for our temporary guardroom, a few logs placed one on the other a little way back. Here we waited till the Grand Rounds came along. Then we learned that one of the sentries near the bank of the river had got excited, fancied he saw some Indians, and was discharging his rifle right along our line. He was at once disarmed, placed under arrest, and taken to the lockup. This same man, long afterwards when on his own farm, imagining he saw Indians in a bluff near his house fired into the bluff killing his own horse.

At first it was arranged to gather all the women in one house with one man to protect them. This arrangement did not please my wife. She refused to go with them and remained in our little shack all alone, I being on guard at night. Previous to this the men on guard had been using the shack as a guardroom at night. The task of removing the men's blankets from the floor and the stuffy air in the place in the morning was too objectionable. My wife preferred to sleep in the shack. If an attack were to be made she had picked out a little hole in the ground—an excuse for a cellar—as a hiding place. Better this than to be huddled up with a lot of screeching women in a house with only one man to protect them!

On the 1st of May a force of about three hundred men, consisting of Police, and troops, proceeded west to punish Poundmaker whose band had been prominent in the depredations that had been committed. Some criticism has been made of the wisdom of this action but those who question it do not realize the effect it had in bringing to account one of the ringleaders of the disturbance and in breaking up his plans of joining forces with the other bands in the rebellion. The force moved out in the afternoon. I watched them from the top of the hill as they took the trail; the Police scouts in advance, the Mounted Police following, and the infantry in wagons. It was intended to make a quick dash. They pulled out about three in the afternoon and engaged the enemy at five the next morning, having marched forty miles by that time.

The story of the Cut Knife Creek fight has been told by others. I did not take part so cannot of my own knowledge relate to this sad story. I am convinced, with all due deference to General Middleton, Colonel Otter, and other military authorities, that had the operations been entrusted to the Mounted Police alone there would not have been the same loss of life. They at least would not have been trapped in a hole. The idea of using a Gatling gun in an affray with Indians that were never known to fight in close order seems to be ridiculous.

The succeeding day was spent by us in anxious suspense. As night approached every man of us was on duty, watching and waiting for news of the results of the sortie. About eleven o'clock there began to be whispers of a fight, of losses, and of a defeat. Towards early morning we could hear the rumbling of the wagons in the distance and later the commands as the force reached barracks and went into camp. Then the officer in his rounds brought us word—eight killed and fifteen wounded. The Indians showed great cunning in picking out the buglers for their aim—two of whom, Paddy Burke of the Police and Foulkes of C Company, had been killed. They knew the buglers sounded the orders and that if these were disposed of there would be confusion.

After this, there was a lull till the arrival of General Middleton with his column. We were prevented from travelling around; in fact there was not any of us hankering very much to go very far from camp, even in the daytime. I got permission one day to go with a team and driver to get some furniture from my house. I found that the house had been used as a guardroom by the troops. The few portable articles the Indians had not carried away or destroyed, the boys had made off with. A long time afterwards several plates of my dinner service turned up, a farmer's wife bringing in butter on them. These had been gotten from the soldiers in exchange for butter! The contents of the writing desk had been scattered on the floor and the boys had evidently amused themselves reading the letters, some of which were from my wife before our marriage! Even my cookstove had been carried off. I found it in the camp being used for cooking by one of the companies from Toronto. The Captain of this Company, Miller, I think his name was, promised that it would be returned to me. Alas, this necessary piece of furniture was loaded on board the steamer when the troops left and I never saw it again.

When I got back to camp with a few sticks of furniture, my wife could not believe that that was all that was left. After questioning me regarding this and that article she had to be contented. The realization of the complete and entire loss of everything evidently sank into her mind with such force that she was left without words to express herself. She accepted the situation. It was no use worrying; the worst that could have happened in material losses had taken place. Thankfulness in that our lives were spared took the place of recrimination and helped to soften the blow. She was never heard to bemoan the loss of the valuable personal belongings—articles surrounded with memories of affection for dear ones who had departed, articles that were gone forever from our possession. Many a time I have felt thankful to God that I was blessed with a helpmate who could survive such a blow with the spirit of resignation that she maintained.

The transport service had a gay time going through the cache of our goods left on the Swift Current trail. One day after Colonel Otter's arrival a long string of wagons came in with supplies. Every teamster was wearing a fine new cowboy hat, all after the same pattern. They had evidently broached a case of our spring hats! Long afterwards we heard stories of how these teamsters had helped themselves to anything they fancied. One man told me he had been offered a bolt of fine silk for a plug of tobacco.

I made particular enquiries endeavouring to recover my wife's wedding dress. It was profusely trimmed with expensive lace which an uncle
had brought from abroad and it was this lace particularly that we wanted to get. We got word of the squaw who took it from the house. She had
bartered it to another squaw who had sold it to a Half-breed woman who
went to Duck Lake. Then I lost track of it. A Half-breed woman who was
doing some work in the house had her child rolled up in a part of a Paisley
shawl and when my wife recognized it she took it off the child and put it
in the stove, so mad was she! We recovered some ivory handled silver
fruit knives. These were found by an Indian Agent in an Indian tepee.
The knives, not being sharp, had been filed down one side like a chisel.

General Middleton arrived from Prince Albert on the 24th of May
with his force on the steamer. Soon after his arrival the Home Guard
companies were relieved from duty and my career as a soldier ended. The
Home Guards as soldiers were a homely looking squad: men of all sizes
dressed in nondescript clothing. Drill was seldom indulged in and when
it was the result was ludicrous. I was in a squad when a sergeant, a farmer,
was endeavouring to put us through a simple movement. He shouted
"take a step to the front with your front foot and a step to the left with
your hind foot." The order so flabbergasted the "awkward squad" that we
all convulsed with laughter. He at once gave order of dismissal! In spite
of appearances there was not doubt of their earnestness, courage, and
endurance had there been occasion to test them in a conflict with the
enemy. We paraded one day for inspection by an officer of the Queen's
Own. We had been only a few minutes before him when he threw up this
hand saying, "take them away! take them away"!

Near the camp of the Queen's Own was pitched a large marquee. It
contained hospital supplies donated by the lady friends of the volunteers
from Winnipeg, Toronto, and Quebec. An officer one day showed me
what was in it! All kinds of fancy groceries, preserved fruits, biscuits,
cases of wine, spirits, a lot of woolen gloves, and other articles of clothing. It was a tempting display for one that had been subsisting for two
months on the coarsest of fare—a strong guard was over it day and
night! In spite of this, cases of purloining occurred every other day. In
the disturbed state of the country such as we were passing through, it

James Clinkskill's store at Battleford

Clinkskill home at 152 Spadina Crescent East, built c. 1903, shown before any landscaping occurred (except fencing). This house became the Armoury duing World War I, and was demolished in 1960.

Left: James Clinkskill, c. 1895 (SAB RB 1355).
Right: A charming picture of Clinkskill as an elderly man, enjoying an outing, c. 1930
(PHOTO LH 2926 6 COURTESY OF THE SASKATOON PUBLIC LIBRARY LOCAL HISTORY ROOM)

Left: Mrs. James Clinkskill (née Babbington Taylor), in Glasgow, Scotland, 1887
(PHOTO LH 2928 1 COURTESY OF THE SASKATOON PUBLIC LIBRARY LOCAL HISTORY ROOM).

Right: Mrs. Clinkskill, c. 1895 (SAB RB 1356)

James Clinkskill seated in his den at home, c. 1911.

Clinkskill home, showing living room with piano, oriental rugs, stained glass window, framed paintings, chairs, etc. Dining room also visible with window seat set into bay window, 1911.

The Duke of Connaught (right), with James Clinkskill and mounted armour guard in background during vice-regal visit to Saskatoon, September 2, 1912.

Celebration of decision to establish the University of Saskatchewan in Saskatoon, 1909. Left to right: Hon. A.P. McNab, Governors W.J. Bell and James Clinkskill, Mayor W. Hopkins.

Left: Studio portrait of Mrs. Clinskill and five of her children, c. late 1880s (PHOTO LH 2927 2 BY DANIEL CADZOW COURTESY OF THE SASKATOON PUBLIC LIBRARY LOCAL HISTORY ROOM)

Right: James Clinkskill, with two of his children, no date (PHOTO LH 2926 3 COURTESY OF THE SASKATOON PUBLIC LIBRARY LOCAL HISTORY ROOM)

A certificate from 1926 showing that Mr. Clinkskill had been accepted as a life member of the Masons.

Composite photograph of the eight children of Mr. and Mrs. James Clinkskill: Grace, Margaret, Georgina, Jean, Tom, Josephine, Louise, Dora, c. 1916.

M C TOMLINSON
CITY CLERK

ALL COMMUNICATIONS TO BE ADDRESSED
TO THE CITY CLERK

CITY OF SASKATOON

Office of the City Clerk

FILE No._____
SUBJECT

Saskatoon, Sask.

Aug. 18, 1936.

Mrs. B. Wood,
1054 Spadina Crescent E.,
Saskatoon, Sask.

Dear Mrs. Wood:-

The Council at its meeting held on 17th inst.
passed the following resolution:-

"That the Council records its deep sorrow
at the death of Ex-Mayor James Clinkskill, one of the
pioneers of this City. The late Mr. Clinkskill took
a very prominent part in the movement to incorporate
the City of Saskatoon in the year 1906 and was its
first Mayor. Both in his private and public life he has
rendered most valuable public services. In his death
the City suffers the loss of one of its most highly
honored and respected citizens. The Council tenders to
the family of the late Mr. Clinkskill its sincere
sympathy and condolence."

At this time I wish to convey to you the
sympathy of myself and fellow workers in your bereave-
ment.

Yours truly,

E. Johnston

Acting City Clerk.

PHOTO LH 2527 COURTESY OF THE SASKATOON PUBLIC LIBRARY LOCAL HISTORY ROOM

*Letter to Mrs. B. Wood (likely Clinkskill's daughter), regarding a council meeting
resolution that it records its sorrow on the death of Mr. Clinkskill.*

PHOTO BY NIGEL P. FRANCIS AND PATRICIA HANBIDGE

Interestingly, the Clinkskill and Mahaffy families shared a common funeral plot and gravestone, in Woodlawn Cemetery, Saskatoon. The photos show the front and back sides of the gravestone.

was surprising how one's perception of "meum and teum" became blunted. You had to keep guard over your belongings with careful watchfulness or you very soon would be stripped of everything. A little pony I had, that my wife used to drive and which was running loose on the prairie near our camping ground, got so abused by some of the troops riding it continually that it died. The General, whilst on the river, received a letter from Poundmaker dated Eagle Hills, May 19, 1885, to the following effect:

Sir:

I am camped with my people at the east end of the Eagle Hills, where I am met with the news of the surrender of Riel. No letter came with the news, so I cannot tell how far it may be true. I send some of my men to you to learn the truth, and the terms of peace, and hope you will deal kindly with them. I and my people wish you to send us the terms of peace in writing, so that we may be under no misunderstanding, from which so much trouble arises. We have twenty-one prisoners whom we have tried to treat well in every respect.

With greetings,
Poundmaker. (His X mark)

The following reply was sent:

Poundmaker.

I have utterly defeated the Half-breeds and Indians at Batoche and have made prisoners of Riel and most of his council. I have made no terms with them, neither will I make terms with you.

I have enough men to destroy you and your people, or at least drive you away to starve and will do so unless you bring in the teams you took and yourself and councillors with your arms to meet me at Battleford on May 26th. I am glad you have treated the prisoners well and have released them.

Fred Middleton, Major General

On Monday the whole of Poundmaker's band with the Half-breeds who had stayed in his camp, calling themselves his prisoners, came into our camp. Two men, one a Half-breed and the other an Indian, came in advance to report that Poundmaker was just behind, coming in to surrender. He was on horseback and after greeting the officers and shaking hands with them, without dismounting—the councillors with him all dismounted before saluting—the whole bunch was conducted across the Battle River to a ridge. Here the Indians sat on the ground in a semi-circle with General Middleton, the officer commanding. Haytor Reed, a number of officers, and other officials were facing them. Poundmaker was dressed in full war costume: his cap was of bearskin, with long feathers standing out behind; a buckskin jacket with brass nails decorating it and almost covered with coloured beads; the usual leather leggings, with masses of beads; light coloured moccasins; and a coloured blanket, loosely on his shoulders. The other Indians wore their war uniform and all were very profusely painted in bright colours. The Chief advanced to the centre and gave a long harangue which was interpreted by Peter Hourie, the official interpreter for the Indian Department. It was quite a poetical speech, principally pleading that he had intended no harm. His young men were carried away with excitement caused from stories of the fighting at Batoche, etc. He had treated all his prisoners kindly. He was unable to control his young men and he hoped he would be given honourable terms. The General's reply was very short and very sarcastic. He ordered them to give up the murderer of Freemont (Barney Freeman as we called him) and Payne. First one came forward, "Man-without-blood," who confessed to murdering Freemont. Then another, "Itka," confessed to Payne's murder. Poundmaker, four of his councillors and the two confessed murderers were arrested for trial; the others returned to their camp. Looking at the crowd of Indians and contrasting their appearance with that described by Fenimore Cooper, one could see how the race had deteriorated. The only one among them that had a semblance to the ideal was the Chief. He was tall, with the good features of the true Indian type and carried himself with a princely bearing. All of them, when speaking, used gestures that could make you almost understand the intent of their words.

The Half-breed prisoners had with them several wagon loads of furs. Looking at these furs, I strongly suspected that our fur collection was amongst them. The furs were deposited in the stores at the barracks. What became of these valuable skins was the subject of much acrimonious discussion in Parliament and General Middleton and other officials were subjected to much criticism. Who eventually got the loot I am unable to state but I have my suspicions! I applied to get a bearskin to make a robe (I had lost five beautiful Buffalo robes) but I was gruffly refused even a look at them.

Before the surrender the Indians had captured a transport train consisting of twenty wagons drawn by oxen. The drivers were made prisoners and kept in camp till the news had been received by the Indians of the complete rout of the Half-breeds and the capture of Riel. They told the tale of the remarkable effect this news had brought about. Instead of the bravado shown at the time of the teamsters' capture, and their threats of killing these men, the Indians now were eager to show a peaceful attitude, hiding their arms and endeavouring to make it assume the appearance of an ordinary travelling camp. The Half-breeds with them, calling themselves prisoners—prisoners who took charge of the camp, engaging in all the deliberations, searching the teamsters at the time of their capture—then changed their tactics. They decided to become loyal, agreed to liberate the captives, and to proceed into town to learn what terms would be granted their associates. Four wagons came in flying the white flag. In it were the teamsters, five of the Half-breeds, Father Cochin, a captured scout, and two Half-breed women. They were willing to promise anything if they were left free. Poundmaker was made the mouthpiece of their proposition to come in and treat for peace. There being no one authorized to treat with them at that time, they went back.

Having disposed of Poundmaker and his gang, General Middleton now directed his attention to getting Big Bear into subjection. As I do not pose as a historian of the rebellion but am simply recording my own recollections of what took place in the vicinity of Battleford and with which I was in touch, suffice it to say that Big Bear and his satellites were eventually captured but only after an arduous campaign of great suffering to the troops. The whole sad story of the repression of the rebellion is just an example of muddle on the part of the military authorities tackling an enemy in their own country and adopting tactics entirely at variance with the experience of Indian fighters. Every fight that took place was practically a defeat. The loss of so many brave volunteers and the hardships that hundreds of men had to undergo would have been avoided had the Police, familiar with the country and knowing every phase of the Indian character, been given a free hand. In bringing to a close this narrative of my experiences during this exciting period I desire to place on record my humble tribute to that magnificent force, the Royal North-West Mounted Police. We who lived amongst them can best appreciate the work which was done. These men with military training but still allowed an initiative of their own in dealing with the Indians, have rendered a service to the country that can never be thoroughly realized. It is considered by those best able to judge that had the force at the outset been given a free hand, the rebellion would have been quelled sooner and with much less bloodshed. I am glad to see that the traditions of the Force are being kept alive and its services in the Yukon, under different yet as dangerous and difficult circumstances, are devoted to the same strict sense of duty.

The noble "Riders of the Plains," God bless them.

Chapter Three:
Politics, 1886 to 1899

NOW THAT WE WERE RELIEVED FROM ANXIETY as to our personal safety, we had to consider our position as a business firm. Our principal store building was destroyed along with its contents. Only a few goods remained in a new building which had lately been constructed on the site of the new town, adjoining the barracks, and we had only a small sum of money on hand with large obligations for goods destroyed in the store and on the trail. We were in a bad fix. My partner went to Winnipeg to interview our creditors. He was well received and generously treated. We had a good, legitimate claim against the goverment but this could not be realized for some time. They proposed to accept an assignment of our claim in payment of our indebtedness and agreed to await a settlement with the government without interest. They also offered us, on time, all the goods we required to go into business again. It was truly a generous offer and was immediately accepted by us. I never forgot the kindness of those houses and up to the time of my going out of the general merchandise business continued purchasing from them.

We experienced great difficulty in obtaining freighters to transport our goods as all our local freighters had lost their ponies. Those that had not been captured were scattered all over the prairie and so we had to look elsewhere for freighters. The price we had to pay was extremely high. The scarcity of available outfits and the sense of danger still existing put the price up. Eventually we got some but had to pay $5.00 per hundred pounds. This, added to the railroad freight of $2.85, ran up the cost tremendously. Of course as is usual, the ultimate consumer had to pay the price. The demand was for supplies and cost did not figure in the matter at all. Some traders anticipating the demand, had through their connections outside rushed in supplies before we could get ours in. They did a tremendous trade, selling out the goods as fast as the wagons were unloaded. Just consider the situation; every one of our settlers was in want of food, clothing, shoes, crockery, house furnishings, everything for a home. Besides there was a large body of Police, two troops and a lot of volunteers who had to be supplied with their everyday needs outside of the rations.

The trade we did for the next two years was enormous, only limited by our ability to buy and transport. Our store building had to be enlarged and new storehouses built. We had to supply our customers with goods on credit as they had no money but, like ourselves, had a claim against the government. Many of them cleared off their accounts when paid for their losses but some black sheep never paid us a cent. A peculiar feature about accounts with us was that the people who owed us accounts for supplies given before the trouble seemed to consider that the rebellion cleared off old scores. Of the thousands of dollars owing to us at the outbreak, we never collected a penny. We had to have a wide margin of profit or we could not have survived.

The government promptly appointed a commission to consider the claims for losses. This commission arrived and held meetings at which the claimants appeared and lodged their claims. Evidence was taken supporting the claims, some which were made up in an extraordinary manner. The amount of work ahead of the commission was so enormous and the necessity of the claimants so pressing that the following spring the government paid one-third of the amount of each claim (outside of business claims) before again holding meetings and taking further evidence. In making up our claim for losses connected with the store we were fortunately placed. Early in March we had taken an inventory preparatory to making a balance. The original sheets had been added up in pencil only. These we put in as the basis of the claim, adding what had been received since and deducting our sales. The commission in dealing with the claims gave peculiar decisions. For instance, in considering the item for carts belonging to our freighting outfit, there were some new carts and some we had purchased second hand. We valued them accordingly but the whole were put down by the commission at one value, that of the oldest cart. It gave us no allowance for a large quantity of potatoes we had stored at one of the reserves. These potatoes were taken and used by the troops but the item was struck out. Then again, the furs which our trader, George Dill, had bartered for goods at Frog Lake were not allowed and only the original cost of the goods furnished in the first place were paid for. Altogether our claim was reduced by eight thousand dollars. We had no recourse and had to accept the amount the commission passed on. As for the claims for household losses by settlers and farmers, these were recommended to be paid on a basis of two-thirds of the amount of each claim and let go at that. Had I been in a position to fight the decision I would have done so. But being broke, and with the necessity before me of having to work day and night trying to make up for what I had lost, made me accept the situation. One of the commissioners, a regular nickel-pincher (what Carlyle would have called "a poor miserable wretched creature") from Eastern Canada, went round the back doors in the village listening to all the old wives' gossip about the character of some of the claimants. He was totally unfit to be entrusted with so important a mission. During all the exciting times the editor of the *Saskatchewan Herald* (our local newspaper) endeavoured to get out the paper occasionally. In the issue of 8th June 1885, he says:

> We will publish the paper in its present shape [single sheet] weekly or as often as we can during the campaign, or until an improvement is practicable. Running a newspaper single-handed and doing military work at the same time is up-hill work.... The rebels and Indians have left us life, hope, and faith in the country, and we do not propose to let the SASKATCHEWAN HERALD go out of existence without a struggle.

This is but an evidence of the feeling of all the settlers. Nothing daunted, they went to work to rebuild their homes satisfied that the future of the country was assured. The land was there as before, the opportunities for advancement unimpaired, and, full of hope, they started life over again.

On the 7th July our first child, Dora, was born. We were still living in the little log shack of one room. The nurse was an old Half-breed woman who was stone deaf. When my wife wanted her to attend to the child in the night time, she had to throw a brush or anything handy at her as no shouting could get her attention. It was truly raising a family under difficulties. As there was no other house available I decided to take my wife and child to Winnipeg, furnish a house, and leave them there till winter when we were to start for Scotland to visit our relations. On the 21st August, our child being six weeks old, we made a memorable trip over the prairie to Swift Current. I had procured a buggy with a top to keep off the sun and, with a team and a wagon to carry the camp equipage and our baggage (which was a negligible quantity), we started out. On the second day it started to rain, raining continuously all day, all night, and well into the next day. It was cold and the little child got so hoarse that her crying was more like a frog croaking.

Arriving at the South Branch, we camped about noon and determined to try to reach Swift Current that night. There was a Half-breed freighter camped nearby from whom I hired what I thought was a fresh horse. I started off about two o'clock. We just got on top of the hill, about two miles from camp, and tackled the level stretch toward Swift Current when it began to dawn upon me that I had been deceived regarding the steed. It was a cart horse that would either walk very slowly or, when urged, would kind of gallop, raising its feet but letting them fall in almost the same spot again. Belabouring the beast continuously was necessary to get it to make any progress. Darkness fell and we were still a long way from journey's end. There was no alternative but to keep going, however slow, as all our camp outfit, grub, etc., was left behind at the river. Before reaching Swift Current there was a long flat and a ridge to cross. After travelling some distance on the flat I discovered we were on the wrong trail; I had missed the forks where the trail began to go up on the ridge. Back I retraced our way. It was intensely dark and I was about parched with thirst, so much so that I could scarcely speak. In going up the slight hill the abominable beast backed; backing locked the buggy wheels almost upsetting the rig. I got out and led, or rather hauled, the brute along. My wife was so alarmed she insisted on getting out to walk, too,

carrying the infant. After a while I offered to carry her burden, she leading the horse. Very soon she gave in as it was more labour to do that than
carry the infant. I insisted on her getting into the buggy as the road was
level and in about an hour I saw in the distance the lights of the town. I
got into the buggy and the cunning old brute saw the lights, too, for he
started a nice little trot that soon brought us to the station.

There was a so-called stopping place at the station and after a great
amount of humming and hawing, we got a bed in a room more like a
clothes closet than a bedroom. But not a bite to eat or drink would they
procure for us. It was now after midnight and we were completely played
out. If it had not been for a little brandy I had with me, I think the child
and ourselves would have succumbed. That was the most anxious time I
ever had on the trail, not so much on my account but I feared for the
safety of the young infant. Next afternoon we took the train for
Winnipeg. We soon got a suitable house, bought new furniture, and, after
getting my wife settled down in comfort, I returned to Battleford.

The trial of the Indians guilty of murdering the settlers and others
took place in the fall of this year and on 27th November 1886 eight of
them were hanged at one drop. Three others were reprieved and given
life sentences. Those hanged were:

>Wandering Spirit—murder of Tom Quinn
>Round The Sky—murder of Father Fafard
>Bad Arrow and Miserable Man—murder of Charles Gouin
>Man Without Blood—murder of Bernard Tremont
>Crooked Leg (a Stoney)—murder of James Payne
>Iron Body and Little Bear—murder of George Dill

The day of the hanging I left on the stage for Swift Current. The hang-
man, Robert Hodson, was also a passenger. We camped the first night at
the instructor's house on the Stoney reserve. We all lay with our firearms
handy during that night but there was no disturbance. The Indians were
evidently completely cowed.

On the day after Christmas I left with my wife and child for Great
Britain on a visit to our relations, returning home to Battleford in May
1887. Previous to leaving Battleford I had picked out some lots on the
bank of the Saskatchewan River and made application to the government

to purchase them (the town site of Battleford was owned by the government). I also let a contract to build a house which was to be ready for us when we returned. On getting home I found that the lots I had picked had been reserved for the Roman Catholic Mission so my application was refused and consequently there was no house built. I managed to rent a new house, that a party had erected for renting, in which we lived till our own log house was erected on another site.

During the summer of 1886 there was a severe epidemic of typhoid fever in Battleford. The very dry weather, the presence of so many troops in camp, and the very primitive sanitary arrangements were the cause. And in June, Poundmaker, who had been released from prison some time before, was addressing a large gathering of Blackfoot Indians at Tobacco Creek, near the Blackfoot Crossing, when he burst a blood vessel and died in a few minutes. In a notice of his death a paper said "He was a man of fine physique and commanding appearance but like most of his race he had undermined his constitution by his excesses."

The season of 1886 was very trying to the poor settlers endeavouring to do a little farming again, making a new start. The summer had been so dry that there were practically no crops of any kind. Hay was very scarce and consequently the price of this for a year was high. A man from Regina had tendered and was awarded a contract for 600 tons at $14.70 a ton by the North-West Mounted Police. The awarding of the contract caused quite a flutter amongst the local contractors who declared it was impossible to get the hay to fill the contract, the available hay flats having been all taken up. One man undertook to corner the market, buying up any hay that was for sale. In the end the Police had to call for new bids to get enough to feed their horses and had to pay a higher price. To keep down the consumption of hay the Police put the horses out on herd, doing everything possible to aid the original contractor. This unfortunate incident raised considerable ill feeling between the new Police Commissioner and the Battleford settlers, a state of affairs that had never existed before. The Police and the civilians had always got along very friendly up to this time.

The Dominion Government having made a redistribution of seats, Saskatchewan had its first election for a member to the Federal

Parliament in 1887. On the 21st January 1887, at a convention of Conservatives at Prince Albert, D.H. MacDowell was elected as a candidate to contest the constituency in the approaching election on the 15th March. The Liberal candidate was D. Laird.

The first opportunity to exercise the franchise caused great interest to be aroused amongst the electors. I had not up to this time during my residence in the country taken much interest in political matters. The policies of the parties were not familiar to me and in consequence I was left to decide in the choice of the candidates altogether from a local point of view which man would be best for us as a member rather than from the larger point of view of policy. I decided to support the Conservative candidate because I knew the man personally (the other candidate was a stranger to me) and he, belonging to the party in power, would be more likely to obtain for the district the necessary expenditures we considered should be made. Just here I would point out how important it is to get an elector, on placing his first vote, to vote for the party you support. Take my case: the policy of the Conservatives was very hazy in my mind, further than knowing it advocated protection to home industries. I was not familiar with politics but afterwards, having learned more about it, I had the feeling of having a prejudice to stay with the party I had first chosen even if some details of their actions were not exactly to my liking. Consequently, through success and through failure I have kept my allegiance to the Conservative Party.

I was persuaded to attend a meeting held at Bresaylor just previous to the election. This was a Half-breed settlement and many of these people, the French Half-breeds, did not come in to the barracks with the other settlers at the time of the rebellion, claiming that Poundmaker had made them prisoners. The claim commissioners had not entertained their claims for losses and so they were positively seething with resentment against the Conservative Government. When I consented to attend the meeting I had not expected that I should be called on to speak. The man who persuaded me to go, when the meeting was assembled, was, through an artifice on his part, voted into the chair. I was left as the only supporter of the Conservative candidate and was compelled to speak.

Going up, I had ridden in a Police sleigh with an officer who was going up to inspect the detachment and who asked me to accompany him. After supper at the Police quarters we set out for the meeting place. A bad snowstorm had come on and we could not see the trail. Men were out on the prairie in various directions and as one caught sign of a trail he shouted and we followed up in the direction of the voice. Eventually, in about an hour (going about one mile), we reached the house where the people had gathered. The house was packed with an excited, angry mob of Half-breeds. When I was called on to speak, I was in a decided funk on account of the angry crowd I had to face. It was my first speech from any platform and interruptions occurred every few minutes. One old chap again and again would demand that I restore the horses the Police had taken. I was momentarily expecting to have my block knocked off. It was a relief when it was all over and I was allowed to depart with my skin whole. The friendly feeling between them and myself which existed before the trouble was, I reckon, the thing that was my salvation. The storm was over and when we left after midnight a bright moonlight shone on us as we travelled home.

The method of running an election was a new experience to me. You were expected, in order to keep up the enthusiasm, to have meetings in every little group of settlers. At these meetings it was always looked for that refreshments would be provided—at your expense, of course. Then the women folk had to be kept in good humour, too. To effect this, "puskies" were held. The night before election day there were dances to which all and sundry were invited. At these gatherings it was necessary to have your stalwarts on hand to see that the girls were not enticed away to the opposition dances. If you let the girls go the men were sure to follow and probably would be persuaded to promise their vote the other way. The fun was kept going till morning. After an early breakfast the voters were bundled into wagons and driven to the poll. There was a bodyguard of supporters who accompanied the crowd and kept off the opposing candidate's friends till the votes were cast, before letting the voters loose. Elections were a gay time to this sort of folk.

The following from the *Saskatchewan Herald* of 3rd December 1887 is interesting: "An Indian just in from Manitou or Devil's Lake, about a hundred miles west of Battleford, reports having seen four buffalo and tracked fourteen others in that neighbourhood." This was the last time any buffalo were seen anywhere near. In January of the following year I ate a buffalo steak at the crossing of the South Saskatchewan, the last time I ever tasted this delicacy. After the disappearance of the buffalo, the hunting Indians used deer meat for pemmican, drying the deer meat in the same way that buffalo meat used to be cured. We used to trade large quantities of this dried meat, pemmican, and moose pemmican with berries in it. The pemmican was put up in rawhide sacks and kept an indefinite time. There was no difficulty in selling all we could get of these commodities as many white people and all Half-breeds considered it a toothsome delicacy.

The winter of 1887–88 was very severe wild cold, snow storms, and a great amount of suffering. Poor Tom Mitchell, who was in charge of one of the mail shacks, on returning from a visit to the reserve was overcome with cold and his body was found close to the trail about one mile from his shack. Dressed only in a light travelling costume, he had sat down to rest on a surveyor's mount within sight of his home when the cold suddenly numbed him and he slept away. His underclothing was frozen to his body. A settler near Saskatoon named Mears got lost going from his house to the stable and his body was found a few miles from his home.

On 25th January I left for a trip to Scotland and returned again on 21st April. On my return trip from Swift Current I met a little adventure. I had requisitioned a special outfit to meet me at Swift Current as my return did not hit the time the stage went out. On arriving at the crossing of the South Branch, we found that the ice had just gone out. Still, a quantity of ice was running and the ferry would not be put into commission for a few days. I got into a small, flat-bottomed boat, crossed the water (dodging the well-rotted floating ice) and landed on the cakes on the other shore. Jumping from one cake to another, thinking it was all anchored ice, one cake on which I landed, not quite in the middle, canted up and down I slid into the ice cold water up to my waist. I clung to that cake for dear life and gradually worked my way onto the centre of it. Taking care to keep on the centre of the other blocks, I arrived on dry land. It seemed this ice was floating in a pocket of water formed by a tongue of sand stretching down the river quite a bit from shore. Here I was with my clothes all wet to the waist and a strong, cold wind blowing. Off I started on the run for a ranch about three miles off where I knew I could hire a team to take me through. Arriving at the house I made my deal for the team and, not waiting for my frozen clothes to thaw out, returned at a jog trot to keep up the circulation, got across without mishap and changed my clothing. The next day I felt no bad effects from my dip.

This trail was the regular route the stage travelled. The stopping houses were of the most primitive character. At the river the Russell House was fairly good. It was built partly of logs and frame, was warm, and the landlord put up a meal one could eat. The next one, after leaving the river, was Otter Station or The Devil's Gulch. It had been made by digging out a hole in the sloping bank, with a few boards for walls and poles with straw on top for a roof. Its size was about ten feet by twelve feet. There were four bunks against the wall, one on top of the other. When there were several passengers, the furniture, consisting of a table and a bench to sit on, was put outside and beds were made on the floor. This place was warm, being well made and in a big ravine sheltered from the wind. Some fastidious people found fault with the accommodation on account of the number of mice that would insist on cavorting over your person after you had gone to rest.

On the way to the next station there was a dug-out in a sheltered place with poles and turf for a roof. It was seldom used as it was meant for a refuge in case of a severe storm coming up suddenly. One of the drivers told me of using it once. A blinding snowstorm had arisen, the cold was intense, and so he made for this place. There was a very small entrance and as soon as he had unhitched the horses, he said they got down on the ground like dogs and crept in. There was just room for the team so he lay down beside them, waiting till the storm spent itself, about twelve hours later.

The centre station, near Eagle Creek, was a board shack built in a ravine leading to a good water pool. The contractors kept the spare horses at this place and it was here that the team drawing the stage was changed. Charlie, a Swede, was in charge and he was a good man for his employers, looking after the stock, keeping them on herd, taking off the shoes before turning them out, then shoeing them again before they went on the road. Charlie was quite a character—when you stopped at his place he talked incessantly and the stories he used to relate in his broken English were most amusing. His stories of the trades he made with passengers passing through was an especially funny theme. There was a story of various kinds of "vatches" he had traded with Jewish pedlars that I have listened to on my various trips. Each time I heard the stories, they seemed to be more amusing than ever. Many years later poor Charlie met with a very suspicious end. After the contractors were changed (on the other route, Battleford to Saskatoon), he took up a ranch, had a good herd of cattle and some horses, married a wife, and settled down. One morning, starting out for Saskatoon, he took suddenly ill and died on the trail a short distance from his shack. There were dark suspicions around. It was known that he and his wife were not so happily mated as they might have been and having a quantity of strychnine on hand for gopher poisoning, it was whispered that possibly he had taken some of it unawares. However, it was never thoroughly investigated and soon was forgotten.

The next stopping place was the Sixty Mile Bush Station, built in the only stretch of timber on the trail. It was a log house, fairly large, belonging to an old chap named Bernier, a French-Canadian. The old fellow had some sense of decency, having little partitions erected around the cubicles to make it better for the lady passengers' comfort. Every time I would stop there he would tell me that "he call for his wife" but "she no come." It seemed she was running a boardinghouse in some village in "Kebec." I fancy the old lady was better off where she was than with him, sixty miles from the nearest town. A great catastrophe happened to him—a skunk had got in underneath the floor and the usual odour after a visit from such gentry permeated the house for a long time afterwards. He resented very much any reference to the subject, although the moment you entered the odour took your breath. A long time after I remarked to him that the bad smell had almost gone and he indignantly replied there was nothing of the kind. He said "one of the drivers lay in that corner (pointing to a corner of the floor) one night and said he smelled a skunk; I tell him he smell himself." Why, even the food he served up tasted of it for long afterwards.

Some horseman passing through sold him a horse that was wild and unbroken. In telling of it, he would relate: "he say, I tie him up tonight, he be all quiet tomorrow. Yes, he very quiet in the morning—he dead." His house got burned down one night, just about when the last few trips the stage made on this route, and he later drifted off to British Columbia. We had been supplying him with provisions and he was always quite a bit in debt. When the stage changed routes, he had some dispute with the mail driver over an account so he refused to pay our account. I fancy he imagined we had something to do with the matter as we were agents at Battleford for the contractor. A long time after, about eleven years, the parish priest in Battleford paid the account on his behalf. The old man's conscience had been bothering him so he sent the money to the priest to pay us. The next stopping place was on the Indian reserve where one had a clean bed and a decent meal. Next "spell" we reached home.

One trip I made over this trail was marked by a little adventure that is impressed on my memory. We had a stoutly built pony, called Fly, in our freighting outfit that was a fairly good driver. I took this pony to make a trip to Swift Current and all went well going down. On the return trip, when about halfway between the river and Otter Station, it had rained shortly before and with the long flat of heavy, alkali land before me, which was very sticky after a rain and made for hard drawing, I stopped, intending to give Fly a feed of oats before tackling the flat. I got out the sack of oats, placed it on the ground in front of him—with the top open—and foolishly took the bit out of his mouth without unhitching him from the buggy. He went on feeding for a few minutes and all at once looked up, snorted, and started off on the run. I leaped for his head, got hold of the bridle, and ran along side. I could not make him stop and after running for about a mile I found it impossible to run any longer. Forcing his head round so that he would be running in the direction I wanted to go, toward the other station, I let him go. I stood looking at him cavorting over the prairie, conjuring in my mind what I was going to do. On the buggy were my blankets and grub. I figured it would be two days before the stage was due at the next station, at which place there was no one stopping and no provisions. And it was twelve miles distant. My heart went into my boots. Watching him in the far distance, I saw him gradually going slower and slower till at last he came down to a walk. I walked quickly along the trail, which took a winding course, and to my delight saw that he, too, was on the trail. I soon caught up to the buggy but no sooner did he see me than off he went again, as fast as he could go. After a while he slowed down and I again caught up. Off he went again. This performance was repeated several times until at last I managed to catch hold of the buggy. I crawled into the back, thinking he might as well draw me in the rig as not. But this would not do—as he ran along the trail, the wheels threw up big clods of mud that rained down on my head. I dropped off and let him go. When he began to feel tired of running, he slowed down and I quietly crept up, seized his head, and managed to put the bit in his mouth. When I was settled in the seat with the reins in my hands, I debated with myself whether I would give him a good licking or not. Looking at the long stretch of heavy trail ahead of me, and considering the supply of oats for his feed was five or six miles behind on the trail, I decided to spare him—remembering I had about a hundred and fifty miles to drive before reaching home. He was a mean brute and I sold him shortly afterwards.

The stage drivers were of the opinion that the "boss" always sent them the wild horses that could not be used on the other stage lines. They certainly were a lot of wild creatures. Before starting, the passengers had to get into the rig while the horses were being harnessed. The driver, watching the animals carefully, then took his seat. Generally, a performance took place—front feet up in the air, then the hind feet, frantic plunges to the side, starting off at a run for a mile or two, and then settling down to a jog trot. The passengers, during this "turn," held onto the seat like grim death. One horse in particular that they used for a while was a peach. After the usual bucking and rearing, he would sit down on his haunches and wait awhile. There was no use urging him. When he was good and ready, and he thought the driver was off his guard, the horse made a wild plunge forward and went off like the wind. It was a wonder to me that there were not some serious accidents.

At the last session of Parliament an amendment to *The North West Territories Act* was passed providing for a legislative assembly elected by the people. The old North West Council was a body partly elected and partly appointed by the government. The appointed members being in the majority, nothing antagonistic to the views of government was enacted. The new assembly gave responsible government but not in the full measure desired by the people as voiced by their representatives.

Early in June the writ for election to the Assembly was issued with nominations on the 23rd June 1888 and the election to take place the 30th June. This election had been looked forward to for some time. One individual, D.L. Clink, had long had an eye for the position and had been strengthening himself with the electors in every possible way. To a large number, however, he was not acceptable so there was a strong feeling against allowing him to be elected. A public meeting was called on the 2nd June in a hall for the purpose of choosing a candidate. The man I refer to, Clink, immediately refused to allow his name to be submitted, saying that he intended to be a candidate whether the meeting wanted him or not.

Several names were proposed, mine amongst them (although I was indifferent in the matter). Ballots were taken of all the names time and again to test which would be the one to gain strongest support. In every ballot my name headed the list. I tried to get out of it but eventually agreed to become a candidate. Some of the friends of P.G. Laurie, one of the men whose name had been submitted, were very sore about my being selected and agreed to the result with very bad grace. Immediately I set to work on my personal canvas, held a meeting or two, and was finding great encouragement. Gradually I began to suspect a coolness in some of my supporters who should have shown greater enthusiasm. Finally I was told that two or three of them were expressing doubt as to my success. This information stung me to the quick. I felt there was no use going on with a contest when your own supporters were so halfhearted in the cause. I went to my committee rooms and informed those there that I was out of the running. I told them to take down the sign and shut up the place, giving them very plainly to understand the reasons for my actions and naming the men who were the cause. There was consternation in the camp; they knew that no other one could put up as good a fight as I could against the obnoxious self-seeker.

I went on attending to my business, paying no more attention to the election. Shortly after this the opposition candidate held an evening meeting to which I did not go. As the evening went on, one man after another came into my office telling me of the hard things my opponent was saying about me and that I ought to go up and answer him. One told me he had called me a coward and claimed that I had received so many rebuffs that I was afraid to go on with the contest. Finally I agreed to go and hear for myself. My opponent was not speaking but one of his chief supporters, J.M. Skelton, a man to me personally very objectionable, was holding forth in somewhat the same strain as my friends had told me about. After he was through I asked if I would be allowed to say a few words. Approaching the end of the room where the speakers were sitting, I was received with jeers of derision from some of the crowd. I began to speak quite calmly and warming up as I accused them of speaking in a disparaging way after I was out of the fight, the Scotch blood rushing to my head as taunt after taunt was thrown at me. I lifted my hand for silence and then told them in quiet, even tones that, so far as being afraid of the result was concerned and in spite of the rebuff they said I had received, I would again take up the fight and dared them to prevent me from heading the poll on 30th June. The meeting became a perfect bedlam. I was surrounded and hustled out to the street and the men went running in all directions shouting "Jamie's out again," cheering and holloing. Half the population of the town never went to bed that night, the excitement was so intense.

The next morning I gathered a lot of my friends together and told them of the tough proposition we were up against. In a contest like this, where party affiliations are not predominant, a great deal depends on the personality of the candidates. By my withdrawal I had lost some who originally intended to vote for me and who, when I was out, had pledged themselves to my opponent. We had to work hard. Those who had been wavering before were the most enthusiastic now. They had been whipped into line in fear of the other man being elected. The other side produced a stylograph sheet called the *Little Joker*. Our side brought out one called the *Big Joker*. These sheets contained all sorts of skits and flashes of so-called humour. I started off to canvas outlying electors, covering marvellous distances and getting little sleep till I had covered the whole district.

I received great encouragement. One settlement, however, Bresaylor, was decidedly hostile. It comprised a lot of votes and, seeing it was little use to spend much time there, I left it to some of my earnest supporters to try and wean away as many as possible.

The night before the election I went over the lists and marked off each man as I had sized him up. What a lot of surprises you get on election day! It was open voting (not by ballot) so we knew how each elector had cast his vote. As near as I could figure it out we should have a majority of 42, after giving the other side all the doubtfuls. Election day came at last. I had all my agents and scrutineers at the various polling places, watching for the unqualified. They headed off quite a number. The other side tried to poll a lot of Indians, some of whom could not even say the man's name but who wanted to vote for the man with the big beard. Some of the returning officers played low down on me. My opponent's name was Clink and when a man was slow in pronouncing my name, before the voter got out the second syllable, the returning officer had already marked it down to Clink. The polls closed and from the results it was evident I was elected in a majority of 24. My opponent lost his head, upbraided his own supporters, and blamed the Police boys for defeating him. He behaved so badly that he lost the little popularity he ever possessed. After the final count was made by the returning officer, I had 180 votes and my opponent 156. There were 74 absentees or aliens that had been on our lists who did not vote. Thus I was thrust into the position of representing a district covering sixty thousand square miles in a legislature of which I was entirely ignorant, either of its constitution or powers. I had everything to learn.

The season of 1888 was favourable and the settlers were rewarded with good returns. As there were a large number of bears roaming near the town, the settlers kept their children safe at home. The milk house of one of the farmers was visited frequently, with all the butter and cream being devoured. Some of the town's boys volunteered to watch for mister bruin and the farmer did not object. Two of the boys climbed on top of the milk house and as the night advanced they became drowsy. One of them, with his legs hanging over the edge of the roof, was awakened by something rubbing his legs. Looking up, there was the bear. Jumping up, thoroughly frightened, he let drive a shot which alarmed the brute and it fled. Another shot or two did not seem to hit any vital part. In the morning his trail was found and traced for some distance by the blood marks but the carcass was not discovered.

The first Legislative Assembly was opened on 1st November 1888 by Lieutenant-Governor Joseph Royal with all due pomp. The escort was supplied by the Mounted Police and, as a wag put it, the band played *God Save The Queen* in both languages. The election of the Speaker took quite a long time. The candidates were H.C. Wilson of Edmonton and James H. Ross of Moose Jaw. Ballot after ballot was taken resulting invariably in a tie. As the Lieutenant-Governor and all the people gathered to see the opening were awaiting election of the Speaker, it was decided to break the tie and, one member having reversed his ballot, Wilson was elected. The first Assembly consisted of twenty-two elected members and three legal experts appointed by the Dominion Government who took part in debate but were not allowed to vote.[1]

Being ignorant of the constitution of Canadian legislative bodies, I went to work studying *The British North America Act* and *The North West Territories Act* so that I could follow intelligently the proceedings of the Assembly. The work of the first Session was largely taken up with discussing an ordinance consolidating ordinances which had been passed in former years by the North West Council. This ordinance had been drawn up by Judge Richardson and A.E. Forget who had been appointed as a commission for that purpose. One of the most important chapters was the *School Ordinance*. In drawing up this particular chapter, in order that

---

1. The members were F.W.G. Haultain (Macleod), James H. Ross (Moose Jaw), Hugh St. Q. Cayley and John Lineham (Calgary),Thomas Tweed (Medicine Hat), Frank Oliver and H.C. Wilson (Edmonton), Joel Reaman (Wallace), A.G. Thorburn (Whitewood), J.G. Turriff (Souris), B.P. Richardson (Wolseley), D.F. Jelly (North Regina), John Secord (South Regina), J.R. Neff (Moosomin), William Sutherland (North Qu'Appelle), R.G. Brett (Red Deer), William Plaxton and J.R. Betts (Prince Albert), Hillyard Mitchell (Batoche), James Hoey (Kinistino), James Clinkskill (Battleford), and George S. Davidson (South Qu'Appelle). The legal experts were Judges Hugh Richardson, J.F. MacLeod, and C.B. Rouleau. Only a few of the members were known to me but the three legal experts I had met frequently before, Judge Rouleau particularly, he having resided at Battleford at one time.

there might be no error in regard to separate schools, the actual words of *The North West Territories Act* were used. The section was passed as in the bill after a long discussion and debate. In the address of His Honour in opening the House were the following paragraphs:

> A statement of the Receipts and Expenditures of the General Revenue Fund will be submitted to you, with the Auditor's Report.
>
> I will also cause to be laid before you, at an early period, the Territorial Estimates for the year 1888–89 which will be prepared with the assistance of my Advisory Council, due regard being had to economy and the requirements of the Public Service.
>
> In the progressive evolution of our present constitution towards thoroughly representative Government, you will find I am in full accord with your legitimate aspirations.

With these words addressed to us, we took the stand that we were to be consulted in the expenditure of all revenues. This view was further strengthened when, in due course, F.W.G. Haultain as chief of the advisory council presented the estimates for 1888–89. The revenue from Dominion sources were included and, in giving assent to this bill, His Honour used the following words: "His Honor, the Lieutenant-Governor doth thank Her Majesty's dutiful and loyal subjects, accepts their benevolence and assents to this bill in Her Majesty's name."

This being the time-honoured form as used in all British parliaments, we construed as definite proof of our contention for control of all revenue from whatever source as desired by the Assembly. However, after the Assembly was prorogued Lieutenant-Governor Royal refused to be bound by the wishes of the advisory committee and maintained that he alone had control of the revenue from the Dominion Government. This reading of the Act led to discussion and friction immediately became acute between the Lieutenant-Governor and the advisory council. At the following Session the struggle for full responsible government and full financial control of all revenues commenced in earnest.

In this Legislature were some very talented members, men who at a later date became prominent in the political world of Canada. I look back with pleasure at the proceedings which then took place and feel thankful for the privilege I enjoyed in being associated with these men. Listening to the debates in which such men as Haultain, Ross, Oliver, Turriff, and Brett were prominent gave me an insight into constitutional questions which was invaluable to me and which could not have been obtained by desultory study. During this Session I tendered and had passed resolutions to be forwarded to the Dominion Parliament urging the old questions of Half-breed claims and for further consideration of claims for rebellion losses made by some parties which had been disallowed. In 1892 the government took action in regard to the Half-breed claims by giving notice to all concerned to lodge their individual claims before May 1894. Many applied and were given consideration with the result that a large number of scrips were issued. The question of licences to sell liquor was also debated and the Legislature was divided on the subject. One party advocated that a plebiscite of the people be taken on the question which was defeated, largely on account of a decision by the legal experts that such a measure was unconstitutional.

Lieutenant-Governor Royal was of a most jovial nature and during the strenuous struggle we were making for further powers he maintained a suave and amiable manner throughout. A dinner at Government House was a delightful function and it was pleasant to watch his genial smile which seemed to grow and expand as the wine circulated. Early in December the Legislature was prorogued and I returned home.

I found speaking in the House a very different proposition from a platform address amongst my constituents. At first I was distinctly nervous. I realized I was talking to a score of men who were familiar with the subject and were probably better posted than I. It was necessary to be quite sure of your facts and to be prepared to back up your statements with authorities. When on the stump, you can be more fluent and even perpetrate a bluff on your opponent at times. Not in the House: mere bluff simply makes one ridiculous. It was a long time before I conquered my nervousness and became able to speak with any fluency.

In May of the following year, 1889, Lieutenant-Governor Royal visited Battleford. The journey from Edmonton was made on the river in a scow. A large party met him at Bresaylor settlement where he landed. Police teams with an escort brought him into town. In the evening I gave a dinner in his honour at which the principal representatives of the town were present. He stayed at my house while his aide and the rest of the party were quartered at the Police barracks. The next forenoon he was presented with an address in English and another from his compatriots in French. In the afternoon a picnic was held on the slope of a hill south of the town. Everybody and his wife was present and there were great doings. An immense fire was built and an ox roasted whole. When it was supposed to be cooked, His Honour cut off the first slice of meat. It was a great occasion and was long remembered by some poor Half-breeds who feasted on the roasted carcass. It was a genuine barbecue. The next day he embarked for Prince Albert.

For some years the people of Prince Albert had been clamouring for railway communication. Their nearest railway point was Qu'Appelle, 280 miles distant, and they became so frenzied about it that they were threatening riots. The government became at last aroused to do something and so made a land grant to the Qu'Appelle, Long Lake and Saskatchewan Railway. It also guaranteed an annual subsidy for a term of years for carrying the mail. On 25th June I received the following telegram: "Start made here today by surveyors on Long Lake Railroad" signed J. Royal. On 17th August the following telegram was received: "Regina congratulates Battleford on building of Regina, Long Lake and Saskatoon Railway. First sod turned today by [Edgar] Dewdney amid great enthusiasm." I sent this reply: "The ancient capital joins with the modern in rejoicing at prospect of being brought together. May the sods go on being turned till the Eden of the North West has been reached." The building of this road would mean cutting our overland travel from two hundred to ninety miles. To us such a distance was comparatively negligible as we considered when Saskatoon had been reached by the railway that we were quite close to civilization. In September of this year the following paragraph appeared in the *Saskatchewan Herald*:

> A private telegram received by a gentleman in town last week brought the gratifying news that the Great North West Central Railway has got out of its difficulties and work of construction would begin at once. The Contract is let to build it to Battleford and fifty miles will be constructed and put in operation this season.

True enough, the line was surveyed and followed practically the route of the original Mackenzie survey of the Canadian Pacific Railway which went through the town of Battleford. The stakes were driven and were in evidence for a great many years but more troubles arose for the Great North West Central Railway and I think that the Canadian Pacific Railway acquired the charter. Our hopes for relief were short-lived and became classed with the many "might have beens" that I have experienced. In 1882 I was assured as a positive fact that a railway would be into our part of the country in two years. I lived in Battleford for seventeen years and then the railway was no nearer than Saskatoon.

The second session of the Legislature opened the 16th October 1889. In the Speech from the Throne at the opening of the House, His Honour dwelt on the fact that there were now 164 schools attended by 4,574 children and taught by a staff of 183 properly qualified teachers. This, of course, covered the whole of the three districts: Saskatchewan, Assiniboia, and Alberta. On the 29th October, Haultain announced to the Assembly, on behalf of the advisory council, that the council had tendered its resignation to His Honour and that it had been accepted.

This action on the part of the advisory council was anticipated by a question asked of it by Cayley a few days before. It was:

> if they have signified to His Honor the Lieutenant-Governor their wish to be allowed, as his advisors in matters of finance, to prepare in conjunction with him, as the Advisory Council, the Estimates for the year 1889–90 to be submitted to the Government, and to submit the same to the Assembly before being submitted to the Government?

To which question Mr. Haultain replied:

> that the Council had not expressed any such wish to His Honor, but that His Honor was in the habit of asking assistance of the Council in the preparation of the Estimates, that the Estimates being purely a departmental affair, His Honor could not consent to their publication to the Assembly, or otherwise, pending their transmission to the Minister of the Interior.

From the foregoing it will be seen that the point of contention between His Honour and the Assembly was that His Honour considered that he was responsible to the Dominion Government through the Minister of the Interior for the expenditure of revenue from federal grants and that the advisory council would not be held responsible to the Assembly for that over which it exercised no control. On the resignation of the advisory council, His Honour selected four other members of the Assembly who were willing to accept office on His Honour's terms. On the 2nd November 1889 the following members were selected as an advisory council: R.G. Brett (Red Deer), J.R. Betts (Prince Albert), D.F. Jelly (North Regina, a member of the first council), and B.P. Richardson (Wolseley). Brett, on behalf of the advisory council, made a statement to the Assembly on 5th November that: "The Council of His Honor's Advisers, formed under the law, will exercise the functions of an Executive in matters affecting the Territorial Finances only," thus giving in to the claim of His Honour and entirely at variance with the wishes of the majority of the Assembly. From this date began "war to the knife." The majority convened a caucus at which it was decided to move a want of confidence motion in the new council and I was selected to make the motion, seconded by Thorburn:

> That the position assumed by the Advisory Council, as set out in the statement of their leader, when announcing the same, was assumed contrary to the wishes of this Assembly, and the Advisory Council do not possess the confidence of this Assembly.

A long debate ensued and a vote taken resulted in the motion being carried by thirteen for and eight against the motion.

After an adverse vote of such decisive weight, under parliamentary usage there was no alternative but for the advisory council under Brett's leadership to resign, which was done. Following the usual procedure in parliament when a government is defeated by a want of confidence motion, His Honour called upon me as mover of the resolution to assist him in selecting another council. A caucus was held of the majority members which, after discussion, laid down the conditions on which we would consent to accept office. Tweed, Neff, Cayley, and myself were chosen to interview His Honour to discuss terms before we would consent to act. The interview continued all day and the result was His Honour would not yield on the important point of the federal revenue.

All our talk was a repetition, each of us arguing on the same grounds. It was like talking in a circle, always resulting in His Honour agreeing to consult the advisory council but not binding himself to be bound by the advice it might tender. In no case would he submit estimates to the Assembly until such had been approved by the Minister of the Interior and definitely fixed without the Assembly having the right to alter them. We parted no further on than when we met.

When we were having lunch, the four of us together, we received an intimation in a roundabout way that if we could see our way to give in to the wishes of His Honour it was quite possible that our various constituencies would receive generous consideration when the distribution of grants for improvements were being gone into. The vast extent of territory covering our different districts and the call for improvement in trails, bridging of creeks, etc., was so large and our total amount of money available being so restricted that it made the proposition a very tempting one. The energy of every member was devoted to getting as large an appropriation for his district as he possibly could. Had we taken action as suggested, the votes with the support His Honour already had in the Assembly would have given him a majority and everything would have been plain sailing for him. However, we scorned the idea and simply laughed the proposition away. I felt sorry in a way for His Honour; his sympathies were with us but the restraining hand of government was so firm that he had to act simply as a buffer between two opposing forces. Failing to get another council to act, His Honour fell back on Dr. Brett to assist him.

The general business of the Assembly continued to be conducted in the discussion of many matters appertaining to the welfare of the country and no sacrifice was made of public interests. A very important memorial was passed urging the Dominion Government to set apart lands for the endowment of a university, particularly pointing out the necessity of doing so before the best portions of land had become alienated to railways or other large corporations. We this early foresaw the necessity of providing for university purposes but I regret to say our memorial did not have the effect desired as no action was taken on it.

A very voluminous memorial was drawn up for presentation to the government dealing with various matters affecting the Territories. The principal matters dealt with, of course, the unsatisfactory status of the Assembly regarding control of federal grants and the amount of these was dealt with at some length. We contended that the total amount voted, $176,410.00, was totally inadequate for our needs and was very much less than we were entitled to. The advisory council in due course brought down the estimates for 1889–90 containing Territorial revenues only. These we refused to pass. In it was an amount of $500.00 to aid in establishing a ferry over the Saskatchewan River at Battleford, an amount thrown out as bait to catch my vote. I had been urging His Honour to make a grant for this purpose and it was put in the estimates with the purpose of trying me out. Should I vote against the estimates, it might be used against me in my district. However, I was not going to be influenced by a paltry grant of $500.00 to sacrifice my vote on a principle. I succeeded a year afterwards in getting out of His Honour, in the last days of his regime, a grant sufficient to establish a steam ferry at that point.

After a session of strenuous debate, the House was prorogued on the 22nd November and in his closing address His Honour used the following words:

> The various incidents, which followed the resignation of my first Advisory Council, the attitude assumed by a majority of the Members, and the earnest desire of all that the business of the Country should not suffer in consequence, are circumstances which will tend to mark this Session as an historical one. I earnestly hope that the proceedings of the Assembly may result favourably for the peace, order and prosperity of the North-West Territories.

So we all went home and when we assembled for the third Session we settled down to the struggle with greater vigour than ever.

The winter of 1889–90 was very severe with long stretches of cold weather and heavy snow falls. In January 1890 we were two weeks without mail. The stage left Swift Current one day behind time and the driver managed to struggle through to Otter Station. Leaving there, a bad snowstorm came up which completely filled the track and every little distance shovels had to be resorted to, to enable the sleigh to get through. Two passengers were along who had to work for their passage and the intense cold added to the difficulty of travelling. When at last the centre station, Eagle Creek, was reached they decided to stay there where there was some shelter. Six days passed before they got away from there. Twice attempts were made to leave but both times the awful condition of the prairie covered with snowdrifts compelled them to return as the trail could not be followed. The third time they succeeded in getting along and soon met relief teams that had been sent out to search for them. These teams having broken the trail, they all got in at last. This was the last winter that the stage travelled this route. The railway being in operation to Saskatoon, the following summer a new route was established. It was a great change as the distance was only ninety miles, which we thought was nothing. When the railway reached Saskatoon it also made a wonderful change for the settlers there who seemed to have taken a new lease on life. Instead of having to draw all supplies from Moose Jaw, over 150 miles distant, they had them brought to their town by rail. The *Saskatchewan Herald* of 11 June 1890 had a little rub at them: "Saskatoon is beginning to move ahead since it became a railroad town. Nearly every house is either a store or a boarding house."

At Prince Albert there was a great squabble about the location of the railway station. On account of the grade, it could not be placed where people wanted it put. The people in this town seemed always to be in a ferment about something. They agitated long about getting a railway till at last it got to such a pitch that almost open rebellion was threatened. The outpourings were of such a frenzied nature, it was said, that Sir John A. Macdonald asked at the time, "Do these people mean all they say?" Eventually the government gave the Qu'Appelle, Long Lake and Saskatchewan Railway a land grant and a subsidy of eighty thousand dollars yearly, for many years, for carrying the mail and government supplies and the railroad was constructed. Another time, when the government telegraph line was extended to Prince Albert, the location of the office displeased them. The men constructing the line were interfered with; poles erected during the day were taken down in the night time and removed. Superintendent Gisborne was run out of town and a condition of rioting ensued. Their point was gained in the end and an additional office was placed to suit the objectors. There subsisted great rivalry between two factions owing to there being two town sites: Prince Albert, the centre of the old, established business section, and Goshen, a subdivision of the Hudson's Bay Company's property at the east end of town.

In the summer of 1890 a new industry for the Half-breeds arose. On the plains, within reach of Saskatoon, there was an immense quantity of buffalo bones strewn across the prairie. In some places, where in former days there had been camps at which great killings had taken place and pemmican and dried meats were prepared, the ground was practically white with bleached bones. These the Half-breeds collected, taking their loads to Saskatoon to sell to dealers who paid $8.00 and $9.00 a ton for the bones. It was no unusual sight to see fifty or sixty cords of these stacked up at the station awaiting shipment. One of the principal trails out of Saskatoon today is called "The Bone Trail," having got the name from the days when this industry was flourishing. The bones were shipped to the United States and used for making char, the smaller pieces being ground for fertilizer.

The 29th October 1890 saw the third session of the first Legislative Assembly opened with due pomp and ceremonies. This session stands out as being the most strenuous and unprecedented in its actions of any constitutional body I have any knowledge of. The advisory council, of which Brett was the chief, continued in office during the recess and took their seats as such on the re-assembling of the Legislature, in spite of the fact that they had only a small following. The day before the opening a caucus was held of the thirteen members composing the majority of the House. At this meeting it was decided that we should undertake to run all the business of the House, ignoring the minority and not allowing them to carry any motion that might be proposed by any of their members. Every evening we met in a room in the original Windsor Hotel and arranged for the business to be done the ensuing day. This coterie was called "The Clan-na-Gael."

The Speech from the Throne was a formidable document for length, touching on a great many subjects, but with no reference to the question at issue between the Lieutenant-Governor and the majority of the Assembly. The first motion by Brett, seconded by Hoey, was "That the thanks of this House be tendered to His Honor the Lieutenant-Governor for the Speech, with which he has been graciously pleased to open the present Session, and that Mr. Speaker be requested to convey same to His Honor." In amendment, Haultain moved, seconded by Davidson, that all the words after "that" to the end of the question be struck out and the following substituted: "The Speech of His Honor the Lieutenant-Governor to this House be taken into consideration on the next sitting day of the House." Voting taking place, the amendment carried. This was the opening shot of the war between the two factions.

The next motion, for appointment of standing committees, met the same fate. The committee to nominate was selected from the majority and the committees were all selected from the majority, not a single member of the minority being selected to act. The next day it was ordered on motion by Haultain, seconded by Tweed, "That Messrs. Clinkskill, Cayley, Neff, and the mover and seconder be a special committee to prepare and report a draft reply to the speech of His Honor the Lieutenant-Governor to this House."

On the 10th November the address in reply to His Honour's speech was presented. This was drawn up in caucus, Frank Oliver being one who was prominent in suggesting the matter of it. This was a plain statement of the position we had taken. The insufficiency of the fund in aid of schools and the retention of part of the grant furnished us with an indisputable argument. We took this means of informing His Honour and of debating the question as it was the only form in which we could publicly present our views. The motion was debated fully, continuing all day till half past three the next morning. On the 14th November His Honour sent a message to the House in reply to our address in reply to his speech. In this message His Honour took up some of the points which we made and repeated what he formerly conveyed to us as his reading of the Act regarding finances. He quoted the report of the Honourable Minister of Justice of 6th January 1890 in support of his attitude, namely, that the advisory council could only deal with Territorial revenues. He also related the resignation of the first council, his endeavour to get a council from amongst the majority members, without success, and his continuing Dr. Brett's council as the only recourse. The address in reply to His Honour's message of 14th November was a most voluminous document and too lengthy to be reproduced here. After reciting authorities of the various *North West Acts* to substantiate our contentions, the following paragraph occurs to uphold our claim for control of finances:

> The Assembly bases its claim to control: 1st, on the intent expressed in plain terms by the title of the vote in Parliament; 2nd, on the necessities of the case, as it affects the people of these Territories through the legislation of this Assembly; and 3rd, on the absolute right of the people of the North-West Territories—according to the scheme of Confederation—to the full control of their own funds.

This ended our controversy with His Honour. Having vindicated the right of the majority of the House to rule, having taken every constitutional means in our power to assert that right, and having taken the precaution that the general good of the Territories was safeguarded by passing useful, necessary legislation, the work of the Session ended. The firm attitude of the House and the unanswerable arguments deduced had their effect. Before the next Session of the Legislature was convened an amendment to *The North West Territories Act* was passed by the Federal Government and our claim for control of finances—full responsible government—was conceded. I may say that in debating this subject the three judges who sat with us as legal experts took no part and in fact absented themselves from the House.

This Session of the Legislature stands out as a most important one in the history of the North West Territories. The struggle for the rights of the people, through their representatives, to full responsible government and the extreme measures taken to emphasize that right, furnishes an episode peculiarly interesting in Canadian history. I enjoyed the work of this Session immensely. Not only the proceedings in the House but also the close association with minds of no mean order in our "Clan-na-Gael" gave me opportunity of enlarging my views and giving me an insight into constitutional questions that I have since found to be of greatest value to me.

My constituents were well satisfied with the stand I had taken in the Assembly and early in January of 1891 entertained me by holding a banquet in the Albion Hotel at which many flattering remarks were indulged in. By a peculiar coincidence, the chairman became afterwards my opponent in the ensuing election for the second Legislature.

In the spring of 1891 a Half-breed was shot at the house of a farmer in the Eagle Hills. The investigation which resulted brought to light a dreadful state of affairs at that place. A complete plant for manufacturing "moonshine" was discovered. It seems that this plant had been operating for some time on quite a large scale. The man who shot the Half-breed during a drunken orgy was tried and convicted. He gave information that lead to the arrest of the farmer who was also convicted and sentenced to the penitentiary for killing cattle belonging to others.

With a view to expanding our business, we opened another store in Lethbridge. My partner removed there and took charge of it. There was a little boom on there at the time but it suddenly collapsed. Our adventure was not the success we expected and a short time afterwards we sold out to a merchant there.

The elections for the new Legislature were approaching and in August I received a strong requisition asking me to stand for re-election. I was at first averse to accepting the nomination as my business, since my partner had gone to Lethbridge, needed all my attention. In the end, more on account of my aversion to the party who aspired to take my place than any desire I felt for the position, I consented to stand again. This proved to be a very bitter contest and was fought by my opponent, J.M. Skelton, on Dominion party lines. I repudiated any claim on the part of Conservatives to support me as such, some of whom voted against me. In my address to the electors was a paragraph that had a very far reaching effect. A very large number of the electors were Roman Catholics and many of them were my warm supporters. To please them, I put in my address the following: "In the matter of Separate Schools, I will use my utmost endeavour to have the present system continued." Not that I did not believe in public schools but as I was representing a largely Catholic constituency I agreed to forward their interest in that regard, just in the same way an attorney would plead for a client. My Protestant supporters were indifferent on the question. When the day of voting came, I regret to say, very few Catholics voted for me. There was no difficulty knowing this as the voting was not by ballot but by open voting. However, on election day, 7th November 1891, I was returned and by an increased majority. The final count gave me 32 of a majority over my opponent.

As portraying the enthusiasm and eagerness of my supporters during this election, the following incident will give evidence. I was west at Fort Pitt, visiting the electors there, and one night during my absence my wife was awakened by a noise outside the house. She arose and going downstairs was alarmed at hearing a crash of broken glass. She shouted "Who is there?" A voice replied, "It is me, John." "Well, John, whoever you are, get away out of this or you will be sorry," she replied. Then a sound of hurrying feet was heard and, looking out a window, she saw several men scrambling into a buckboard and, in their haste and tipsiness, knocking each other off the rig. It afterwards transpired that they had not come to frighten her, as she supposed, but John, who was an ardent supporter of mine, had brought the crowd to see me as he had persuaded them and they had promised to vote for me. Needless to say, they were all Half-breeds.

After the election was over, my opponent was so disgruntled and disappointed at the result that he filed a petition of protest against my return. The petition had some twenty-nine charges and I fancy they were formed on mere rumours and his disordered imagination because he did not follow it up but let it drop. The result of the election was a bitter disappointment to him. He had been so sanguine of success his family had prepared a great feast for the evening of the election. They turned out to be the "baked meats" for his political funeral. On our side there was great jubilation and a torchlight procession, of which I was the centre in a buggy drawn by rope, round the town to my house, much to the consternation of my little children who thought the men had come to burn down the house. A lot of money changed hands over the result as there had been a great deal of wagering going on. One bet had a rather amusing conclusion. Two old chaps, one of them an Irishman and Pat Maskell, a great friend of mine, had bet fifty dollars against a wagon belonging to the other. My friend went to get the wagon and took it over to his yard, amidst the tearftil remonstrances of the owner. In the night time, the former owner of the wagon went over and removed the nuts off the wheels!

Pat Maskell, referred to above, was a warm-hearted old fellow who was very grateful to our firm. We had outfitted him with a horse, harness, wagon, and provisions to enable him to take a contract from the government telegraph department which yielded him a large profit. He took particular interest in my family and meeting my wife in the store one day, when he had been having a drop of "crathur," insisted on buying a shirt for her boy. "He knew how it was. When he was a boy there was only one shirt in the family and the first up in the morning got the shirt." He wanted to be sure that her boy had a shirt all to himself. When hard pressed for a drink (it was prohibition days), Pat would call at my house hoping to be offered a dram. On the occasion of one of these visits he had quietly pocketed the bottle, after which my wife would take care that only a decanter was in sight. Pat was hurt in his feelings and expressed himself thus: "Now, Madam, you know well enough I can't put the decanter in my pocket." My wife said, "Wait a minute, Pat," and, going to the kitchen, filled a bottle with tea and gave it to him. It so happened the tea had not been quite cold and Pat, taking it to put in his pocket, felt the warmth and looking reprovingly at her said, "I thought you gave it to me too willingly."

The summons calling the meeting of the Assembly was delayed in reaching me on account of the heavy snowfall making travelling very slow. The stage was two days late in getting to Battleford. The date of the meeting was the 10th December and I received my letter on the 7th, giving me a very short time to get to Regina. There had been another heavy fall of snow after the stage had passed over the trail which meant that the road had to be opened again. I hired a man who had a heavy team of horses and we took the front bobs off a heavy sleigh, fixing a square box on top, and with this strong outfit we started. The horses never went beyond a walk as the snow was very deep and all the trail was blocked. By travelling night and day, simply stopping to feed the team at the stopping places, we arrived at Saskatoon just as the train was about to start for Regina. I went aboard the train, not having time to get a meal or change my apparel. In my haste I forgot all about my baggage till we were well on the road to Regina. I was dressed in my travelling outfit—moose skin coat, moccasins, etc.,—not quite presentable for "company." On arriving at Regina I had to buy a complete new turn-out from the skin out. It was a week before my baggage got to Regina.

When the second Legislature met on the 10th December 1891 it proved to be a long Session, lasting till the 25th January 1892. A large amount of work was done and a number of very important ordinances were introduced and passed. This Legislature is distinguished as witnessing during its course a struggle between two factions, not on any question of principle but on the rather sordid desire for office. I regret exceedingly to record that my action at the end of the first Session furnished an excuse to base the contest upon and I cannot say I feel any pride in the part I was forced to take in the struggle which ensued. The judges no longer sat with the Assembly as legal experts. The opening took place on the 10th December 1891 with the usual pomp and ceremonies. James H. Ross of Moose Jaw was elected Speaker. The Speech from the Throne by His Honour, amongst many other matters, announced to the Assembly as follows:

> By virtue of an Act passed last Session by the Parliament of Canada, it is enacted that this Legislature shall, subject to certain provisions, have power to make Ordinances in relation to various subjects, and, amongst others, the expenditure of Territorial Funds *and such portions of any monies appropriated by the Parliament for the Territories* [Clinkskill's emphasis] as the Lieutenant-Governor is authorized to expend by and with the advice of the Legislative Assembly, or of any Committee thereof.

I can imagine the pleasure it gave His Honour to announce to us the complete surrender on the part of the Dominion Government to our demands which we so firmly claimed and with such unanswerable arguments presented our case. He no longer was placed in the position of buffer between the government and the Assembly but could now be in peaceful accord with the majority of the House.

In framing the amendments to *The North West Territories Act* the government deemed it unwise to abolish the advisory council. During the period of passing the Act and the election of a new Legislature, there would of necessity be occasion for the Lieutenant-Governor-in-Council to exercise certain functions to carry on the ordinary business of the Territories as laid down in the several ordinances. So Parliament left the matter to the Assembly to legislate as to what "committee thereof" should be created for that purpose. On the 24th December an ordinance, which had been introduced by Haultain, was passed entitled "An Ordinance respecting the Executive Government of the Territories" providing for an executive committee consisting of four members. The members selected were Haultain, Tweed, Neff, and myself.

The amended Act gave us power to legislate in respect to the sale of intoxicating liquors and accordingly a Bill was introduced by Cayley, the discussion of which occupied a great deal of the time of the Session. During the recess for Christmas I, being compelled to remain in Regina as the period of adjournment did not admit of my going home to Battleford, assisted Cayley to draw up his Bill. The work consisted largely in cutting out portions of the *Manitoba Act* and the *Ontario Act* and pruning them to suit the conditions of the West. The resolution was again passed urging a larger appropriation of monies for the North West Territories. The main contention was that we ought to receive, instead of an annual vote of an indefinite sum, a fixed amount in the nature of a subsidy and giving the considerations on which we thought it should be based. These financial resolutions were passed time and again but it was not till the question of provincial status was broached (many years after this date) that any heed was given to our contention.

There was a great deal of hard, conscientious work done during the Session. It was free from any discussions between the Assembly and the executive committee. Haultain was leader and, of course, introduced all the government bills. A great deal of time had been taken up discussing a school ordinance introduced by D. Mowatt of South Regina. A few days before the wind up of the Session this ordinance was dropped. To provide for the grants in aid of schools it became necessary to pass an ordinance for this purpose. Haultain had the bill prepared without consulting any other members of the executive committee. In this bill, besides providing for aid, was a clause to the effect that all schools be subject to uniform inspection. Here was a dilemma for me to face. With the recollection of my election address in mind, in which I had made the pledge that "In the matter of Separate Schools, I will use my utmost endeavour to have the present system continued," I was confronted with the choice of two courses—either to vote against the clause, and in so doing vote against the executive committee of which I was a member, or to vote in favour of it and swallow my pledge. I did not hesitate one moment as to what course I would pursue. I seconded an amendment against the clause and immediately intimated my resignation from the committee. The question was presented to me so suddenly it astounded me. The clause in itself seemed so innocent that very few of the members realized that the suggested change struck at one of the first principles of separate schools. Had this bill been discussed by the executive committee before being presented in the House, there would have been some way of arranging the matter to enable me to support the financial clauses and vote against the obnoxious clause which I could not vote for and retain my self-respect. I was strongly pressed to reconsider my decision of resigning but I could not see any other course to take and formally resigned. The afternoon of the same day the House was prorogued.

There was a member of the Assembly who sat in the House for this Session only, Charles Nolin, the member for Batoche and a Half-breed. His election was protested and he was unseated. It seems he had run the election on the day of voting to suit himself. It was proved he had refused to allow some voters to poll their vote, being in the polling place and having ordered the returning officer not to accept their votes. Another charge which was proved was that he made the officials in the polling place proceed to the home of a priest who was too sick to come out and record his vote there!

Charlie was a character. He had been a prominent member of Riel's council in 1885, only withdrawing at the last moment to save his skin. In a debate on the question of having the ordinances printed in the French language, he, speaking in French, made an impassioned speech in favour of it. He claimed that the French people founded the North West and so much was the country saturated with the French language that if the birds of the air and the fish in the lakes could speak, they would do so in French. Governor Royal told us that in the good old days in Manitoba Charlie had been a member of the Legislature and Minister of Agriculture in Royal's cabinet. Charlie said he was not going to resign. He had a good job and nice salary and was going to hold onto it. Charlie was a "Leeberal" in Dominion politics and frequently came to Battleford when a contest was on. He did make some wonderful breaks when speaking for his candidate. I heard him say one time that if the Liberal Government was returned that party would bring back the buffalo! Charlie had been very nervous all Session for fear the petition against his election would be decided before prorogation. However, the Session finished and he drew his indemnity. Mr. Bouchier, also a Half-breed, was elected in his place.

The control of federal funds was in the hands of the Lieutenant-Governor up to the end of 1891. I did a good stroke of business for my district by inducing His Honour to appropriate $2,500.00 to aid in establishing a steam ferry on the North Saskatchewan River at Battleford. There had been correspondence regarding this matter and tenders had been called for but the terms laid down had been such that no one would undertake the proposition. An offer had been made afterwards and submitted to His Honour reminding him of the offer. Following several interviews, he asked me to ascertain if the offer made was still open for acceptance. I wired to Battleford and received an answer in the affirmative. Submitting this reply and urging acceptance as strongly as I could, His Honour eventually agreed to make the grant. This was considered a most unusual concession, our funds at that period being extremely limited, and my success was the envy of the other members when they came to know of it.

On my return home I met a great reception. A procession of sleighs came out to meet the stage, accompanying me into town. The ardour of my friends was cooled somewhat when they learned that I had resigned from the executive committee. Some of them expressed themselves strongly against my action; the majority, however, considered I did the correct thing. A short time afterwards I called a public meeting to explain my action as I considered this was due to my constituents.

Although apparently we had succeeded in gaining financial control of sums voted for the North West Territories, there were still many disputes with the Dominion Government as to the rights of the executive committee to act with the Lieutenant-Governor in various matters connected with the carrying out of the ordinances. Other matters connected with finances, for instance the estimates presented to the government for the year, were prepared by the Lieutenant-Governor without consulting the executive committee. The sums voted by Parliament were voted for specific purposes and were based not on the needs of the country but on the state of the treasury or the caprice of the Minister of the Interior. These and other subjects were debated between them.

In March a man named Wall brought a queer-looking instrument called a phonograph into Battleford. In its then form, the phonograph consisted of a large, round cylinder with a number of tubes leading from it. These tubes you held to your ears and the operator, setting the thing agoing, you heard the record. This was the source of much excitement, nothing like it having been seen before, and the fellow made a lot of money out of his speculation. He charged 25¢ for each "turn" and it went from morning till night, yes, and nearly all night. Some of the boys treated a few Indians to a hearing and, well, their faces were a study. They had nothing to say—all you heard from them was a grunt. A Half-breed told me they thought it was a "Manitou" or devil.

In April 1892 I received word of the death of my father in his eighty-third year. He had been failing for about two years. He had no organic trouble, the doctors said it was simply a weakness of the valves of the heart owing to age. As he expressed himself to me, using a mechanical expression, "the bearings were becoming worn out." So well had he been feeling the day previous to his passing away that he had written me a long letter, which letter I received by the same mail as the intimation of his death.

About the end of May the steam ferry, for which I had succeeded in getting an appropriation, was running across the North Saskatchewan. It was built on the catamaran principle: two boats joined together by the deck with the wheel at the stern working between the two boats. It proved to be a great boon to the settlers, bringing those on the north side and at Jackfish Lake in direct communication with the town. This convenience of crossing the river induced a large number of settlers to locate on the north side where there were large stretches of hay lands around lakes, making it a very desirable location for keeping cattle.

In June I took a trip through that part of my district, investigating conditions of trails, etc., and deciding where improvements were to be carried out. Combining business with pleasure, I took my wife along for the outing. We had a wagon to carry the camp outfit and a man to make camp, cook meals, and provide a little game. Being travellers, we were not prevented from shooting game for the "pot" and had a very pleasant time. We camped whenever we desired and called on my constituents as we travelled along, listening to their wants in the way of improving trails, keeping in touch with their operations, and getting acquainted with the women folk—not a bad stunt to be amiable to the women when elections come round. I found that they, leading a very quiet life, were as much interested in the success of their candidate as those having the vote. It made a subject for them to talk about and broke the monotony of their dreary, isolated existence. The money available for improvement was so limited that nothing could be spared for engineering expenses so I had to do the laying-out of the works, draw plans, make specifications, and inspect the work after completion.

My partner, who had returned from Lethbridge, leaving a manager in charge of the store there, conceived the idea of going into sheep ranching. We engaged a good man to select the stock in Ontario, principally Shropshires, and ship them to Saskatoon. Our flock arrived in Battleford in good shape; we only lost one ram (two rams started fighting with the result that one got his neck broken). These sheep we gave to a rancher to look after but he neglected the care of them with the result that we dropped all the money we had put into the venture. We were greatly disappointed with the outcome of our speculation. The stock was the very best grade (the rams were thoroughbreds) and we had looked forward to introducing sheep-raising among the settlers, to go along with their cattle growing, and increase the prosperity of the community. It was a lesson to us not to depend on anyone else to look after our property. This man was considered one of the best farmers and ranchers in our district, which accentuated our disappointment.

A session was held in August of 1892 which proved to be a memorable one. It was short but exciting. The opposition to Haultain's leadership was, of course, composed of the former members who had been in the minority during the Session of 1890. Cayley (who had ambitions) had gathered a following of his own to oppose Haultain. When the motion for going into supply was made, Betts and Mowatt moved an amendment against the motion which carried 13 to 12. The amendment was based on the fact that the vacancy in the executive committee, owing to my resignation at the end of the last Session, had not been filled till shortly before we met. The amendment expressed dissatisfaction at this tardiness, leaving North Saskatchewan without representation during the recess (it was, in choosing the committee, made desirable that the different areas—north, south, east, and west—should have representation on the committee) and wound up with "and in other respects." This last phrase was the subject of much raillery in the debate which followed. Haultain, being defeated, signified his resignation and that of his colleagues the next day. The Lieutenant-Governor called on Cayley to form a committee. He chose Thomas McKay, D. Mowatt, and Joel Reaman and met the House as leader. The position of the two parties then stood at 13 for Cayley and 12 for Haultain. On Cayley announcing his committee, a most astounding action was taken by Speaker Ross, a proceeding unparalleled in the history of legislative assemblies. He left the Speaker's chair and took his seat on the floor of the House, which then made the parties equal and created a deadlock. Ross, when taking this extreme step, made the following statement and handed it to the Clerk of the Legislative Assembly that it might be recorded in the *Journals of the Legislative Assembly of the North-West Territories Council*:

> In resigning the Chair of this House. ... to which a large majority of those who for two years previously had been struggling for responsible government had been returned; as one of the party which had been engaged in that struggle and had been successful in the late general election, I reasonably expected that any Advisory Council or Committee which might be formed would be composed of those and those only who had belonged to that party. ... In view of the defeat of an Executive advocating the principles which I had struggled for longer than any other Member of this House, and the success of a party evidently, indeed necessarily, opposed to those principles, I feel that in duty to myself and my constituents, I must place myself in such a position as to be able by voice and vote to advocate those principles and protect the interests of those who elected me to this House.

Cayley endeavoured to have William Sutherland of North Qu'Appelle elected Speaker against his desire, he being a supporter of

Haultain. The Clerk declared that the votes being equal, there was no election and left his seat; the members left the House. The next day Cayley repeated his motion but again the votes were equal, 12 to 12. Sutherland and I not being present, as it was expected he would be nominated by Cayley and me by the other side, as a result of the deadlock Cayley threatened that he would have the House prorogued. That evening Haultain interviewed His Honour at the request of some of his supporters and remonstrated with him against the threatened prorogation, intimating that the situation would soon right itself. Haultain had already been informed by some of Cayley's party that they thought matters had gone too far and they were ready to change their vote. This, however, he did not make clearly known to His Honour. Royal was very much upset by the course of events and seemed determined to support Cayley in his stand. The next morning Haultain and two others waited on His Honour and informed him that their party was willing that C.A. Magrath be elected Speaker but His Honour intimated that they were too late and that the proclamation proroguing the House had been signed. There was nothing for us to do but wander home. The only ordinance receiving assent during this Session was one to encourage the planting of trees.

According to proclamation the third Session met on the 7th December 1892. During the recess Reaman, one of Cayley's executive committee, died, which necessitated a by-election. This contest was exciting as on the result depended the fate of Cayley's administration. Both Haultain and Cayley were in the constituency, each fighting for his own candidate. It resulted in the election of F.R. Insinger, the Haultain candidate. When the Assembly met, Ross was reelected Speaker. On the 12th December Haultain moved:

> Resolved, That under the provisions of Sub-section 12 of Section 6, Chapter 22, 54 & 55 Victoria, a Committee of four members of this House be appointed to advise His Honor the Lieutenant-Governor in relation to the expenditure of Territorial Funds and such portion of any moneys appropriated by the Parliament of Canada for the Territories as the Lieutenant-Governor is authorized to expend by and with the advice of the Legislative Assembly or of any Committee thereof.

This being in the exact wording of the clause in the amended *The North West Territories Act*, it will be noticed that this was a change in the procedure of forming an executive. In former occasions the Lieutenant-Governor invited a member to choose his committee; in this case the House passed a motion appointing them. Accordingly, the next day Daniel Campbell moved and Magrath seconded a motion that Haultain, Tweed, Neff, and Mitchell be the committee. An amendment proposed by myself and seconded by Betts to the effect "that the Committee should be so composed that representation shall be given to both parties which have recently existed in this Assembly" was lost and the main motion carried.

Haultain had the majority in the House and he maintained that position during the lifetime of the Legislature, that is till the Territories were divided and the provinces of Saskatchewan and Alberta were established, a period of fourteen years. Thus ended the ambition of Cayley for power. Looking back at the part I was forced to take in aiding and abetting his desire, I feel ashamed and regret that I should have been compelled to side with him in his endeavour. When it is borne in mind how easily the matter of my resignation from Haultain's first committee could have been avoided, the blame for the extraordinary proceedings of the former Session cannot but be placed on Haultain himself. Able, clever, and resourceful as Haultain was, he had a failing of being too apt to consider and decide matters himself, taking for granted that his colleagues would fall in with his views. This was certainly evidenced in the case of the clause regarding schools. Apart from this failing, which wore off in later years, I cannot speak too highly of his ability and his good work for the Territories. To my mind the people in the West do not realize what they owe to him for the work he accomplished on their behalf and for the solid, useful legislation he caused to be enacted. He stands to this day head and shoulders over any man that has taken part in political life in the West. The fact is, he is too much the statesman and too little the politician to suit Canadian ideas.

We dispersed on the last day of the year and I brought in the New Year at Saskatoon. I used to stay at a stopping place kept by a German couple and the old lady had a bedroom, which she considered her best, which was called my room. This night she prepared my bed to make it specially comfortable. The bed tick had been filled with a fresh supply of hay and well tossed up. In the morning my joints seemed to creak as I moved about and were excruciatingly painful. The warmth of my body had melted the frost out of the hay, which had been taken right out of the haystack when the temperature was away below zero, and I had a nice attack of rheumatism in consequence. I refrained from telling her of it for fear she might think me ungrateful.

The whole community of Battleford was saddened by the death of Robert Wyld in June 1893. He was known and respected by everyone. His long connection with the North-West Mounted Police and his business afterwards in ranching and cattle dealing had brought him into touch with everyone in the district. A generous, off-handed method of transacting his affairs had endeared him to all. In his will I was appointed one of the executors along with W.J. Scott, the Registrar of Land Titles. We experienced great difficulty in getting a grasp of his affairs. No regular system had been followed so there were no records on which to base our operations. One transaction involving about seven thousand dollars was recorded in pencil on the back of a large, official envelope.

Bob had been buying cattle from the farmers, putting his brand on the animals, and leaving them in the farmer's care till the animal was fit to ship or kill. Owing to this, his cattle were scattered all over the country. After we had followed up every clue available to find his property, we advertised that anyone having cattle with his brand on them should notify us or take the consequences of being considered being in unlawful possession. We recovered sixty head of which we had no trace. When the cattle buyers came around, I had to be present to take description of the animals sold. It was a beautiful sight as the herd came down the slope of the hill with the cowboys rounding them up and driving them into corrals. At first I was brave and took my place on foot in the corral, picking out the animals. A big, fierce steer charged at me and I made for the fence, climbing up just in time to escape being gored. After that I did my business from a safe vantage on the top of the fence.

In the fall about 200 head were driven down to Saskatoon for shipment on the railway. I went down to make delivery and get payment. The head of the firm, J.T. Gordon, on whose behalf the purchases had been made, was on hand. He started culling out a number as not up to shipping standard. He had just received a cable that the price of cattle at Liverpool had dropped, causing his firm to lose on a big shipment that had just arrived at that market, so he took advantage to select only the very primest steers. I strongly resented this action, claiming that his buyer had selected these cattle, which was not denied. But he simply refused to take them and there I was. After the cattle were loaded and I received payment, there was nothing for it but to drive the remnant back to the ranch. As can be imagined, I guarded against this sort of thing in future deals and insisted on delivery being taken at the ranch. There was not any loss sustained, however, as the next season prices were higher and we more than covered the expense of keeping the cattle over for a season. It took me four years to wind up the estate. Being anxious to realize as much as possible for the heirs, I gradually reduced the herd by selling off the female stock and disposed of the steers as they became saleable at a good price instead of selling the whole herd in bulk. When having my account of the administration passed by the court, the late Judge Richardson complimented me by saying that it was a unique instance of so much more money being realized for the heirs than the testator had left when he died.

A movement was made this summer to erect a memorial to those who had been killed in the Rebellion. It took the form of iron gateways with pillars of native stone and a wire fence around the cemetery. The wire for the fencing was furnished by our firm at actual cost and the lumber for same was supplied by the Prince Brothers at a low cost. A general holiday was proclaimed and a bee was held by the whole town and the fence erected; the gateways and pillars were erected from the proceeds of various entertainments and by subscription.

Times were hard and work was scarce this summer. It was the year of great depression in the United States, the effect of which was felt in the Canadian west as well. Quite a number of men were engaged on the River, panning gold from the gravel beds in the North Saskatchewan from Edmonton as far down as Fort Pitt. We purchased this gold right along from these miners. They told us they made from one to three dollars a day

working at it. It was risky work buying the gold; some of it was not sufficiently calcimed and a certain portion of the quicksilver remained in the
clinker. The gold was found in very fine flakes, called flour gold, and had
to be collected with quicksilver, which was driven off by calcimining.

The death of Judge Macleod occurred in September. His death cast a
gloom over all the West where he was so well known and respected. In
talking over this event, one member of the Assembly who was in the
habit of using "strengthening language" said of him, "the Judge did not
have too great a knowledge of law but he was hell on equity."

On the 17th August 1893 the fourth Session was opened by
Lieutenant-Governor Royal and nothing transpired during this Session
to mar the peaceful work of legislation. The Lieutenant-Governor, when
proroguing the House, in his speech made reference to the changes made
and advances achieved during his regime in the most amiable and generous terms. It closes with the following paragraphs:

> When on the 4th July, 1888, I was sworn in as Lieutenant-
> Governor of the North-West Territories, the functions of that
> Office were as totally different from those of Lieutenant-
> Governors of the Provinces as they will be from those to be
> performed by my successor. I was responsible to the Privy
> Council of Canada alone for all executive acts done in the
> Territories. The Assembly had hardly a voice in the
> Government of the Country and the Lieutenant-Governor
> was practically a Political Commissioner under whose direct
> supervision and authority the affairs of the Territories were
> conducted and administered.
>
> Now all this has been materially changed and hence my
> satisfaction.
>
> The Legislature today practically enjoys the rights and privi-
> leges of self-government. Let me congratulate you sincerely
> upon the wisdom and discretion you have displayed in under-
> taking your new and important duties.

The fifth session of the second Legislature was opened on the 2nd
August 1894 by Lieutenant-Governor C.H. Mackintosh. His Honour's
speech was distinguished only by its length and the variety of subjects
touched upon. The Session lasted from 2nd August to 7th September.

Nothing occurred to disturb the peaceful order of business and a number of useful pieces of legislation were passed. The change in the schools ordinance, changing from a Board of Education comprised of two sections—one Roman Catholic and one Protestant—to a Council of Public Instruction composed of the members of the executive committee—two Protestants and two Roman Catholics—who were nominated. That these nominated members were without vote was the subject of remonstrance on the part of the Roman Catholics through Father Leduc and A.E. Forget, the Catholic members of the Council. The Council of Public Instruction regulated the management and discipline of schools, the examination, grading and licensing of teachers, the selection of textbooks, the inspection of schools and normal training. It will be seen that the whole of the regulations in relation to schools are dependent on the composition of the executive and, as pointed out in the resolution: "the present Executive is composed wholly of Protestants *with little hope of its complexion being changed so long as the numerical proportion of Roman Catholics remain as it is now*" [Clinkskill's emphasis]. The regulation will be framed in accordance with Protestant views but in the efflux of time, should the Roman Catholic denomination become predominant in the executive, or provincial government, the regulation may then be in the hands of a Roman Catholic.

I would point out that in the Act itself no reference is made as to what these regulations should be—they are left entirely to the Council of Public Instruction. It is an Act embodying this principle of the Council which has been embodied in the constitution of the provinces of Saskatchewan and Alberta and must exist for all time. The settlement made in the Dominion Parliament in regard to separate schools was on this basis. Clifford Sifton, who left the government on the question of separate schools of any kind being thrust upon the provinces, dissented from this arrangement. Frank Oliver, after years of struggle in the local House against separate schools, supported it knowing full well the true intent and significance of the Act. The Roman Catholics, whilst being opposed to the measure as being contrary to their desire for full control of their schools, acquiesced unwillingly. But with the usual farsightedness of their denomination they are quietly preparing for the day when, by

means of their numbers and by having their people in the different elec-
toral districts throughout the West, they may be able to control the
Council of Public Instruction and obtain a full measure of satisfaction in
the regulation of their schools. The Liberal Party, which proclaimed far
and wide that this Act would protect the advocates of public schools
from the alleged evils of the provision for separate schools, was guilty of
the vilest hypocrisy and gave the western provinces a stone when they
asked for bread.

In pursuance of my pledge, I perforce had to vote with the Roman
Catholics in discussing and voting on the report of the committee which
had been appointed to report on the resolution's addresses to the
Assembly. The Roman Catholic Papers, and numbers of various pamphlets discussing the question from the Roman Catholic standpoint, were
profuse in their expressions of admiration for the stand I took in the
House. What did it all amount to? In the succeeding election for the
Assembly, not only did they not support me but actually put up one of
their own faith to oppose me!

A new Act was passed at the previous Session providing for election
by ballot and was tried out at a by-election in the district of Whitewood.
The Bill was drawn up and introduced by Frank Oliver and had some
peculiar features. It was based largely on the endeavour to enable every
voter entitled to vote to have the opportunity of doing so. There were no
voters lists provided for. Any voter whose right to vote was challenged
was allowed to mark his ballot but it was put in an envelope on which
was inscribed his name and the reason of the objection to his voting. This
envelope was deposited in the ballot box with the rest of the ballots not
objected to. After the day of voting, but before the returning officer made
the final count of the ballots, a court was held at which evidence was
taken on the objection to the voter. If it were found to be on good
grounds and the objection was upheld, the envelope containing the ballot was destroyed without the marking of the ballot being disclosed. If the
objection was not sustained the ballot was taken from the envelope and
placed with the good ballots in the ballot box. The voter whose right to
vote was challenged was required to sign an affirmation instead of taking
an oath.

The method of voting was by means of a coloured pencil. The ballot was a piece of plain cardboard, the size of two postage stamps with a crease in the middle. The returning officer, having initialled the ballot on the back and having made an impression with a stamp, the device of which was not known till immediately before voting commenced, handed the ballot to the voter who went into the appointed place, made a mark on the inside of the ballot with the colour allotted to the candidate he supported, then closed the ballot at the crease, moistening the gum at the edge of the inside of the ballot to make it secure against detection. The mark was preferably to be an X but any mark of indication of the intent of the voter was permissible. This Act was found to be very cumbersome and defective in many ways and was abandoned in a few years.

The election for the third Legislature was held on the 31st October 1894. I did not require any great pressure to bear on me to be a candidate on this occasion. I was determined to show my independence of the Roman Catholic voters who had failed me at the last election. Immediately after the writ of election was issued I declared myself a candidate. For a few days there was no sign of opposition. In going around I happened on a man whose support I had every reason to expect but he informed me he was undecided whether he would be with me or not. The day after he declared himself in the field. He was a prominent French-Canadian, Ben Price (now a Senator), in good circumstances and with a multitude of relations amongst the voters. One great disadvantage he laboured under was his inability to speak on the platform. The first time I met him after he had declared himself a candidate I suggested we hold joint meetings to minimize travelling around as much as possible. He did not want to arrange this and intimated that probably public meetings would not be to his advantage. He appeared at one meeting I had called in town and, really, his attempt at speaking was so pitiable that it completely disarmed me and I had to leave him alone. At this meeting I made clear my actions in regard to the school matter and frankly told them my views, that I had voted as I did on account of my former pledge, that in future I intended not to be bound to any definite action, and claimed complete independence of any party or denomination.

The morning after this meeting I started for Bresaylor and Onion Lake, in the western part of the district, to address meetings I had arranged for at these places. In the middle of the night messengers roused me out of bed at Bresaylor, informing me that my opponent had gone into my Committee Rooms and told my men there that he had retired and did not intend to continue the contest. I was urged to go back to Battleford at once but I refused. I had called the meeting at Onion Lake and I was bound I would not disappoint the people there, although I was sure the majority at that place was going against me. The journey meant travelling two hundred miles and, being late in October, the weather was decidedly cool. Still, I was determined to keep my appointment.

On the way home I learned at the telegraph station at Fort Pitt that my opponent had changed his mind and was going to see the contest through. At the meeting I had held at Battleford the evening before my departure, a Judge of the Supreme Court had been present. Judge Maguire, who had been holding court, was a Roman Catholic who was much in sympathy with my position. I was informed that he had persuaded my opponent to retire, pointing out to him the ingratitude evidenced in opposing me (in fact, he wrote me to that effect after my opponent had again resumed his canvas). After the departure of the Judge two very bitter opponents of mine, J.M. Skelton and Tom Dewan— one the opposing candidate in my previous election and the other an Irish Roman Catholic and brother-in-law of the present candidate—had remonstrated with him and compelled him to resume the fight. I wrote to Mr. Forget, at that time Commissioner of Indian Affairs, and also to the Roman Catholic Bishop asking for an explanation of why, after their and other Roman Catholic authorities' high commendation of my action, I should be opposed by one of their faith. The answers I received were laughable; they reiterated their compliments while at the same time expressing their inability to interfere.

Nothing daunted, I worked like a beaver day and night canvassing, endeavouring to see every possible voter in the constituency. At Onion Lake, although the voters were not numerous, about 30 altogether, they were decidedly hostile to me. One of my supporters, an English Roman Catholic, decided to go there to be present on polling day. He was at his wit's end to know how to turn the tide. When the poll opened, the first voter, who was for the other side, was foolishly challenged by the scrutineer for the other side. An inspiration came to my friend and he immediately left the poll, went amongst the waiting voters, all Roman Catholics, and informed them that William (the first voter) had been made to take an oath by the scrutineer and made to swear on a Protestant Bible. That trick swung the pendulum the other way. Up they went and voted straight for me. At the close of the poll I had a majority in my favour. On the evening of 31st October I had a majority of 18, the smallest I had yet received but it was a great satisfaction to defeat them, the miserable ingrates.

The Saskatoon Trail, which followed the river closely, required a great deal of work on it. Going from Battleford, in the first twenty-two miles there were eighteen creeks, some with deep descents on each side. I decided to expend my appropriations on improvement of this trail, grading the road and building bridges. I called for tenders and let the job to the lowest tender and had the work completed that fall. The following March a complaint signed by three of my constituents (one, a former opponent at my second election; one, the Irish Roman Catholic brother-in-law of my most recent opponent; and one, a rabid member of the Grit Party) was forwarded to the executive, making charges of misdirection of funds, passing of accounts for work inefficiently executed, etc., based on a report furnished by one of my supposedly warmest supporters. The matter was considered sufficiently important by the executive that it advised the Lieutenant-Governor to appoint Mr. Haultain a Royal Commissioner to investigate the complaint.

Mr. Haultain duly arrived and held his own investigation. The parties were notified to produce the evidence and it was ridiculous to listen to their story. The greater part of it was hearsay and rumour. One charge was that I had paid seventy-five dollars for work that was worth only fifty dollars. After producing evidence of practical men as to the work done and how much they would have done the work for, Mr. Haultain turned the vouchers and showed them that only twenty-five dollars had been paid with the balance going to cancel a debt the contractor owed for seed grain advances. I got work done as a repayment. (I may state here that my district was the only one in which any attempt had been made to collect the cost of seed grain advances.)

Another charge was that in building the abutments of some of the bridges, the specifications had not been followed. The specifications called for dowel pins to be inserted at intersections of the logs composing the abutments. When the witness was asked how he could tell that no dowels were used, his reply was that there were no auger chips on the ground. His inspection took place six months after the work had been completed and a whole winter's snow had fallen. It turned out in evidence that these logs had all been squared and prepared in the bush before being drawn to the site of the work. In another case, they stated that payment had been made to the contractor on some bridge work before enough work had been done to warrant the payment. The voucher was produced which showed that payment had not been made for six months after the contract had been completed. At the succeeding Session of the House, Mr. Haultain reported that there was no shadow of grounds for the complaints. These thrice-defeated opponents of mine were sore losers but I never had any trouble with them again.

A general election for the Dominion Parliament was expected at an early date. Several members of the Assembly were spoken of as probable candidates. There existed some doubt as to the method of a member of the Assembly resigning his seat. Mr. Bourinot, Clerk of the House of Commons and the first authority on parliamentary procedure, gave his opinion that there was no provision enabling a member to resign in order to run for the Federal House. A special Act was passed at Ottawa remedying this defect. Mr. Frank Oliver resigned and was elected for Alberta at the subsequent general election.

A new departure the Indian Department inaugurated in regard to the Indians after the Rebellion was beginning to show the wisdom of the regulation. Each family was furnished a cow and access to "community" bulls was provided. This original cow belonged to the department but any offspring was the property of the individual Indian. When the mature animal was sold by the agent, a cheque for same was sent to the Indian. At first the increase was killed and issued as rations to the band but after a while the increase was so much larger that the steers were sold to cattle buyers. These cattle, being of good grade, well kept, and usually in prime condition, were much sought after and always brought top market price.

Nothing the department ever did in regard to assisting the Indians was successful. An Indian, as a rule, could not grasp the idea of cultivating land, putting his work into a thing, not getting a return for a year, and probably meeting with crop failure, but the cattle idea appealed to him much more favourably. It had the effect of making him work harder and take better care of the animals, knowing that they were positively his property. When a number of cheques arrived, it was a busy time in town attending to the Indians, who were like children and just had to spend the money as soon as it was received. Some of them had amounts from seventy-five to a hundred dollars to spend.

In the fall of 1894 and the following winter, owing to a complete failure of crops, there was widespread destitution and want amongst the settlers along the main line of the railway. Relief works were started and Haultain had a busy time organizing and providing work to give assistance to the suffering. The funds of the Territorial Assembly were used, making us short on our other appropriations for a time. The Dominion Goverment partially repaid us for the expenditure afterwards. In the spring of 1895 seed grain had to be furnished to enable land to be seeded.

In June of 1895 the Indians held a great thirst dance about eight miles from Battleford which attracted a great many spectators. I was very much amused at the advantage taken of the curiosity of the whites, or "Moonias" as the Indians called us. At the entrance to the enclosure where the dance was being held, an Indian was stationed to take the quarter-dollar charged for seeing the show. Having paid your money, following the practice of a railway conductor, he placed a piece of paper in your hatband which gave you run of the camp—quite a bit of civilization. The camp was about two hundred yards in diameter with the one hundred and sixty teepees being placed in a circle. In the centre was a pavilion about forty feet in diameter made by sticking green boughs in the ground and with a screen of boughs at one side behind which the dancers rested between performances. There were fifteen male and ten female dancers. The dance started at six o'clock on a Thursday and continued till Saturday at six o'clock. During this time the dancers kept up their antics without eating, drinking, or sleeping. It was simply a test of endurance. There was no making of braves as this rite had been forbidden by the department. This ancient custom consisted of young men showing their contempt for pain by inserting skewers of wood through the fleshy part of the breast and the body was suspended by the skewers. At one time no young man was considered a brave, or full-grown, man entitled to the privileges of such, till he had undergone the ordeal.

The first session of the third Legislature opened on the 29th August 1895. His Honour's speech was again distinguished for its length and the variety of insignificant subjects dealt with. Of course he had to mention at some length the success of the Territorial Exhibition held at Regina in July. The exhibition was a particular fad with His Honour, he having conceived the idea and took everything to do with seeing it carried out. It cost a great deal more than was expected, the payment of its debt taking a long time before being wiped out.

The session, which was a brief one, was full of useful legislation. Only one little affair ruffled its tranquility: a criticism of Mr. Haultain's distribution of relief to the destitute settlers; but it had no lasting effect. With T. Tweed having resigned from the executive, J.H. Ross was elected in his stead. For the first time the Estimates were voted in detail, a certain sum for a specific purpose. A Department of Public Works was established with local improvements in the different districts being controlled and carried out by officials of the department under Ross as minister. This step was decided in advance and each [district obtained improvements that were necessary, instead of the] amount available being divided equally among the districts.

A new industry was started during this year—the digging of Seneca root by the Half-breeds and others. It was a great boon to them, some families making from three to eight dollars a day. The operation employed the whole family: the men did the digging, the wife and children pulled off the green parts before washing and drying the root. So extensively was this carried on all over the country that it brought down the world's price so much as to make the industry unprofitable. Our firm alone shipped about ten thousand pounds the first summer. The root was fibrous, with roots with the fine tendrils being considered most valuable, the heavy bulbous roots being an objection to the buyers. It was used largely in the preparation of patent medicines, having a slight aperient effect. The taste was astringent and the flavour similar to wintergreen. The plant was easily detected when in flower, similar to a small violet, and found in large patches in moist places. Our Indians would not dig it or allow anyone to dig for it on the reserve. They had a superstition that it was unlucky to disturb what they looked upon as a medicine plant. It was claimed the work was surer pay, less labourious, and more profitable than washing gravel for gold.

Owing to hard times from strikes in the coal mines and the irregularity of demand for coal, our business at Lethbridge was unprofitable and we out sold out the stock to a merchant there and rented the building to a tenant. This was in February 1896. Two of my sisters from Scotland had come out to Canada on a visit. I met them in Winnipeg and together we journeyed to Battleford. The drive from Saskatoon by stage was a unique experience for them. The weather was intensely cold. On leaving Saskatoon the stage driver heated a rock, wrapped it in a sack, placed it at their feet below the robes, and then wrapped the robes tight around them. When we got to Henrietta, the first stopping place, they were quite comfortable. Sitting in the front with the driver I got full benefit of the cold wind and was compelled several times to get out and run to warm myself up. The rest of the journey was more agreeable as the weather moderated. They appreciated the remarks of Baillie Nicol Jarvie, that when you went travelling you could not expect to carry with you "all the comforts of the Sautmarket."

The memorable Dominion Election of 1896 took place on 23rd June. The contest in our constituency, which extended from Onion Lake in the west to Cumberland House in the east, was between three candidates: Wilfrid Laurier, Jas. Mackay and Craig, the last mentioned running as an independent Conservative. Laurier was elected by only 44 votes and had Craig not butted in, Mackay [would] have won easily. The poll at Cumberland House defeated Mackay; the rest of the riding gave him a majority. The figures ran 988, 944 and 213 for Craig. I have often heard it said that speaking at public meetings seldom made votes but after our experience during this election, I formed a different opinion.

A meeting was held at Jackfish Lake, a hotbed of Liberal voters. Mackay and I spoke for the Conservatives while one of my former opponents and Charles Nolin spoke for Laurier. The issue, as will be remembered, was the Remedial Bill on the Manitoba School question. The Liberal speakers betrayed such an ignorance of the fundamental principles of the matter in question that Mackay simply "wiped the floor" with them. Before holding this meeting we estimated a hostile majority of nineteen; on polling day we had a majority of three for Mackay. It turned out to be an all night sederunt with intervals for refreshments being held. Someone stole Tom Dewan's whiskey and then sold it back to him without his suspecting anything. It was a wild night and about daylight as we could not travel the uncertain trail in the dark, we started back for Battleford, well satisfied with our efforts.

After the general result of the election became known, the Liberals becoming the "top dog," they did ride over us in good shape. To be known as a Conservative after that flop-over was a brand of infamy. It was a positive wonder how many claimed to have voted "right" and were hot-foot after the loaves and fishes. Had they all been counted up, it was a marvel how Mackay received any votes at all.

The result, of course, made necessary a by-election. Laurier sat for his Quebec constituency, as he said he had to "stand by Quebec." He never had any intention of representing Saskatchewan, although his supporters had produced evidence before the election that he would if elected. Davis and McPhail, two Prince Albert Liberals, contested the seat with Davis being returned. On the polling day a pathetic scene was enacted in one of the polling booths. A French-Canadian (a good friend of mine, by the way) after receiving his ballot went on his knees asking pardon for voting for a Liberal. That was a good old dyed-in-the-wool Tory for you.

Do what we could, it was impossible to increase our business. The lack of railway communication so long promised and expected was a bar to our getting new settlers. The volume of business was at a standstill and what there was of it was keenly competed for by the three stores. In view of this fact, my partner decided to withdraw from the firm and in July of 1896 we dissolved partnership. I continued the business alone.

The second session of the third Assembly was opened on the 29th September 1896. The speech of His Honour Lieutenant-Governor Mackintosh was again a lengthy document. It was an epitome of the events and progress of the Territories during the preceding year. Owing to the resignation of Frank Oliver, he having been elected to the Dominion Parliament, a by-election took place in August and M. McCauley was elected in his place. I was appointed along with others to prepare a memorial to the Governor-General-in-Council "setting forth the financial and constitutional position of the Assembly, the amendments which should be made to *The North West Territories Act* to secure fuller powers, and the basis upon which the subsidy should be determined." The memorial was a very full definition of our position and suggestions as to amendments to remedy the anomalous standing of the executive committee in relation to executive acts of the Lieutenant-Governor. It is too voluminous to be given at length here but in short, whilst not demanding full provincial status, we urged an amplification of our powers to govern the Territories in a more efficient manner in keeping with full responsible government. The financial portion of the memorial was a reiteration of our former demands for a more liberal subsidy. The House was prorogued on the 30th October.

On the 19th December a by-election in Saskatchewan was held. This election was necessary to fill the seat to which Laurier was elected at the General Election. As he decided to "stand by Quebec," he took his seat as representing a constituency in that province. The Conservatives did not put a candidate in the field so the fight was between two Liberals of Prince Albert: Davis and McPhail, with Davis being elected. This was the entry of the now well-known Senator T.O. Davis into parliamentary life. If all the stories going about the "hail fellow well met" Tom were related, 'twould fill a book. Before this election there were discussions in the Liberal camp at Prince Albert where there was a Davis faction and an anti-Davis group. Tom's brother Joe and he were not very good friends, this antipathy being the outcome of a long-ago business transaction in which Joe claimed Tom got the better of him. When the trouble was at boiling point and a fear was awakened that a Conservative might slip in to the seat between the two factions, Senator Forget, who was then Commissioner of Indian Affairs, happened to be in Prince Albert and approached one of the brothers to smooth matters over. He imagined he was speaking to Tom, who had the government support, and spoke openly about party affairs. It was only after he had got through that he found he was addressing Joe Davis, the insurgent! His discomfiture only can be imagined. He laughed heartily at the incident when relating his mistake to me some time afterwards, adding, however, that there had been nothing said by him to implicate anyone. Tom managed to pull through and was elected by a majority of 154.

This general election and the turning out of the Conservative Party had a very lasting effect on the cordiality of the people of Battleford toward one another. Up to this time there had been a friendliness and sympathy with one another that made a feeling as if all were one family. When local elections came along, each one had their inclination toward one candidate or another and when it was over no hard feeling was engendered. But a difference began to be evident amongst the followers of the Liberal Party. One Conservative official after another was attacked and hounded till his dismissal was accomplished and a Liberal appointed in his stead. The Indian Agent was dismissed on the excuse of negligence, in losing a lot of cattle belonging to the department. The fact was that a terrific prairie fire swept the district and destroyed the hay put up for the cattle late in the season, when no hay could be had to feed them. A French-Canadian, a Liberal, of course, was put in his place—a man who in 1886 had been dismissed from the service for immorality. The land agent had charge after charge laid against him, all of which were proved to be without foundation. When no fault could be proved, the office was closed and the agent informed his services were no longer required. The postmaster was dismissed and a Liberal appointed.

The postmaster, J.B. Mercer, had the satisfaction of giving his persecutors a "Roland for their Oliver." Four of them signed a solemn declaration that he, Mercer, had tampered with the voters' list at the General Election. The four signers were J.M. Skelton, Tom Dewan, C.M. Daunais and W. Latour. Mercer laid information against the three first named for perjury. The fourth, Latour, had come to Mercer and informed him that he had signed the document not knowing its contents and apologized for having done so. The others maintained their action and claimed they could prove their statement was true. After a preliminary trial they were sent up to the Supreme Court for trial. The trials took place and in the cases of Skelton and Dewan the jury found them guilty. In the case of Daunais the jury disagreed. An appeal was made on some technical points but it, too, was dismissed. Skelton and Dewan were sentenced to a short term of imprisonment but released by order of the government after they had served only a few days. The conviction and sentence was all that Mercer desired as it cleared his character. He had no objection to their release. When Daunais came up for another trial, the crown prosecutor informed the court that he was instructed not to proceed with the case. All these incidents embittered the feeling amongst us and the happy family feeling that had formerly existed was dissipated forever.

The Klondike craze, as we called it, struck us this year. In the height of the excitement all sorts of routes were suggested as being the most feasible. Prince Albert and Saskatoon were urging a water route starting north of the North Saskatchewan on some lake which was connected to some other lakes by streams till you reached Athabasca Landing. Some parties actually started, some of them in Peterborough canoes, but none ever proceeded very far. Sealed tins of preserved foods were scattered along the shores of the lakes and were "taken care of" by travelling hunters. Several of our citizens decided to go, some by way of the Pacific coast and some by what was called the overland route via Edmonton. Of all that started by the latter route, only two, J. Rose and E. Rose, father and son, reached Dawson. The latter part of their journey over the mountains on foot and dragging hand sleighs was particularly trying and they underwent great hardships and privations. Of all that went to the goldfields, I know of none that made a fortune.

In the spring of the next year, I sent fifty horses and carts, a freighting outfit I had purchased, to Edmonton to sell to the travellers going north. Most of them were purchased on arrival there by the Police who knew the build of ponies required for work of that kind. After I had despatched my freighting outfit to Edmonton, allowing sufficient time for them to get there, I made a trip to Edmonton overland. I had arranged with Gid Jackson to drive me as he was taking a fine team of driving mares for the purpose of selling them there. The day before we were to leave, Gid received word that his mother, who lived in Ottawa, was very ill and so he decided to go east. I persuaded Jack Mercer to go with me and drive the team, as I would not trust myself with the care of such valuable horses. We left the afternoon of the 22nd May 1898—got as far as Fort Pitt that night. We stayed with the telegraph operator overnight and in the morning drove to Onion Lake, remaining there over the Queen's birthday as guests of the Indian Agent, George Mann. When leaving, Mr. Mann accompanied us a little distance to his cattle camp and showed us the scene of the Frog Lake massacre.

We camped next at the operator's house at Moose Creek. He was not at home but had told us where to find the key to his shack. We got in and made ourselves at home. This was the most lonesome place I ever stayed. In the middle of big spruce brush, perched on the brink of a high cut bank overlooking the creek and with the nearest neighbour forty miles off, it was solitude, no mistake. Starting off early the next morning we made Victoria where we crossed to the south side of the river, following trail till we came to Fort Saskatchewan. After again crossing to the north side, we drove into Edmonton. We made great time, averaging sixty miles a day. The team trotted into Edmonton with their heads up and stepping out as if starting on an exercise drive.

This was my first visit to Edmonton and I was well pleased with the layout and the prospects ahead of it. Both Mercer and I knew a great many people in the town and we were royally entertained. The town was busy outfitting Klondike prospectors. Some of these were queer-looking chaps, all in high spirits looking forward to golden returns. Many of them were not fitted to undertake a trip of a hundred miles on an ordinary trail, let alone a journey of hundreds of miles through swamps, muskegs, and mountain passes. The craze was a harvest to the outfitting firms. I saw one fellow who started for Dawson with his outfit in a big barrel with an axle through the centre being trundled along by six St. Bernard dogs. About ten miles out of the town, he camped, resting for noon. He never got farther on his way than St. Albert, sixteen miles out.

The real estate market was quiet, although the men were active in trying to push business. I was urged to buy a well-located lot for five hundred dollars. Three years afterwards the Bank of Montreal paid eleven thousand for it and today it is valued at two thousand, five hundred dollars a foot frontage. What a chance. I lost it, but I was like the man who was offered the town site of Chicago for a pair of boots but did not have the boots. I did not have five hundred dollars at the time. The outlook for business so impressed my friend Mercer that he decided to tear up stakes in Battleford and locate in Edmonton. After a delightful sojourn of a few days, we started back on our return journey of our hundred miles with a team of cayuse ponies. What a time we had with these animals, pounding them along. What a contrast to our trip up: the mares going a steady gait, taking Mercer all his time holding them in, and now using up gad after gad on the backs of the ponies. About half-way home rain started to fall and continued for two days, making us utterly miserable. Heat I can stand and cold I can endure with equanimity, but rain makes me thoroughly miserable.

The contract for carrying the mail between Saskatoon and Battleford having expired some time ago, the contractors, Leeson & Scott, had been continuing the service on a monthly agreement. This firm being Conservatives, such a condition could not be tolerated any longer. Advertisements were inserted in the newspapers calling for tenders and, of course, a Liberal, Tom Dewan, was awarded the new contract as a reward for his loyalty to the party. In starting the service he ignored the old contractors and refused to purchase any of their plant or even occupy the old stopping places. A new trail was laid out following a route further back from the river and three new stopping places erected. This trail was very rough till it got smoothed down with travel. The freighters gradually adopted this route as it avoided some hilly country near the river, but as it was not on the surveyed trail no permanent improvements could be made with government money.

The passage of the freighting wagons gradually wore down the unevenness and made travelling more comfortable. The stopping places were primitive log shacks with a sod roof on a row of poles. In some of these houses when it rained, the water came through causing great discomfort. Tom was trying to run the business as cheaply as possible. The parties he hired to look after these places were not always suitable and were frequently changed. Consequently the travelling public had to endure the discomfort. The first stopping place, about 22 miles from Battleford, was Buffalo Head, so called on account of a large buffalo bone head having been placed on the ridge of the roof. It was not so bad a place as some of the others. It was built near a running creek of very fine spring water which furnished a supply of good drinking water that could not be had at the other two places. Fortunately, at first the parties in charge were decent white folks who kept the place clean and served up fairly good meals. After a time Dewan sold the place to a farmer, who continued to keep "stoppers" on his own account, who also gave good accommodation. Of course, sleeping places were limited and when there were several passengers (the two stages, one out and one in, stayed over night here) on the stage it was the floor for most of them. The middle station where a change of horses was made was an awful shack. It was called the Red Fox—why? I do not know. Here had one Half-breed family after another looking after it, each succeeding one seeming to be less suited for the job than the last. It was dirty, cold, and positively swarming with insects not mentioned in polite society. I have frequently seen lady passengers sit up all night on a common wooden chair rather than risk undressing in the mysterious curtained-off sleeping places. I invariably lay on the floor with my robes over me without undressing.

At Battleford the Police boys used to give entertainments occasionally. Dewan supplied the provisions for this and the next resting house, paying the parties so much for keeping house. Sometimes in the winter the supply of provisions would run short and consequently the menu would be rather scant. However, the charge for a meal, fifty cents, never varied. One time I stayed there when a whole boiled turnip was the "*pièce de resistance*"—no bread, a miserable hard bannock, no butter, tea without sugar or milk, but the charge was the same fifty cents. A fellow at one time who had charge of this place possessed a disreputable gramophone which he turned on when you arrived and kept going all the evening. When I happened to be along he would insist on grinding out a record of the bagpipes, evidently in honour of my nationality. I insulted him grievously one time, after a particularly harassing record had ceased. I said, it was a fine violin solo. He said, indignantly, "why, that is a coronet solo." So much for my musical discernment.

About twenty-five miles from Saskatoon was the third resting place called the Badger House. It got the name from an incident that occurred shortly after it was built. There happened to be a number of passengers and the table accommodation being limited, it was necessary to have two sittings to serve the party. As the second squad sat down a cattle buyer from Gordon & Ironside, a jocular fellow, in joke said to the "cook" that he would like to have a bit of the badger meat that had been served at the first table. One of the lady passengers, just out from England, on hearing this remark went outside and became actively sick. She imagined she had partaken of some of the badger. The place was dubbed the Badger House ever afterwards. At one time there was a Scot in charge who was a Burns' enthusiast and quoted Burns' works all the evening. About 1902 the then occupant, learning that the shack was a homestead quarter and having a dispute with Dewan, made entry for the homestead. Dewan changed the stopping place to Park, a few miles nearer Saskatoon and on a different trail. This was a farmer's house where clean accommodation was provided and decent meals were served up.

The third session of the third Assembly met on the 28th October 1897. In His Honour's speech he said:

> Since the last meeting of the Legislature important changes
> in the Constitution of the Territories have been made by the
> Act passed at the last Session of the Federal Parliament. In
> accordance with the provisions of that Act I have chosen an
> Executive Council, and can now congratulate the Territories
> upon having obtained a completely responsible system of
> Government.

We had now obtained what we struggled for during the last nine years and enjoyed full responsible government. We still were dissatisfied with our subsidy and this formed the subject of still further memorials. A number of important ordinances were passed during this Session. A memorial was passed urging the Dominion Government to open up an overland route to the Yukon in order that supplies going into that district might be obtained from Canadian sources instead of from the United States, as was the case at that time. It was also decided by the executive council that G.H.V. Bulyea proceed to Dawson to investigate and claim the receipts from liquor permits going into that district. A large number of trained dogs were required for travel up there and I procured upwards of fifty for the government from the Chipewyan Indians at Cold Lake and

Lac la Biche. The dogs I furnished proved to be better than any procured from other sources. The team that carried Mr. Bulyea trotted into Dawson as fast as when starting out and were sold there for more than twice what they had cost. The Mounted Police brought up several cars of Newfoundland dogs but they proved to be unsuitable as their feet played out. The toes, being feathered, had ice form between them and the dogs who were biting the ice off pulled the hair, making the flesh raw and laming them completely. When proroguing the House on the 15th December, His Honour in his speech said:

> During no Session since the creation of the Legislative Assembly has so much and so important legislation been passed.... . The legislation for establishing and organizing the Public Service will, I am sure, enable the business of the *Territories* to be administered in keeping with the larger duties and responsibilities which have been imposed upon you.

In April 1897 a span of the Railway bridge at Saskatoon was carried away when the ice went out. Unfortunately when this happened there was no train or engine on the line at Saskatoon or going north to Prince Albert. There was no train communication north of Saskatoon till the bridge was repaired which took a long time as the material for reconstruction had to be brought from British Columbia. Several four-horse teams came down from Prince Albert carrying mail and passengers. The Battleford mail, passengers, and freight were landed on the east side of the river and taken over on the swing cable ferry. In August 1898 the fourth session of the third Legislative Assembly was opened by Lieutenant-Governor M.C. Cameron in a speech of more moderate length than those of his predecessor. One of the principal items referred to the cutting off of the Yukon and its formation as a separate territory. Also referred to was the comparatively large increase in the revenues caused by the sums collected on liquor permits going into that district. There was little contentious matter introduced and the work of the Session consisted of passing several important ordinances without much controversy, only one division being recorded. A redistribution ordinance was passed providing for two more members in the new Legislature. The House was prorogued on the 17th September by the administrator, Judge Richardson, owing to the illness of Lieutenant-Governor Cameron.

This Session concluded the ten years of my service representing the Battleford district. During that period I had the satisfaction of being identified with the advancement of the Legislature from a form of tute-lage to complete responsible government. I shall always look upon my connection with this development as the most interesting period in my public life.

Chapter Four:
Saskatoon, 1899 to 1912

M Y BUSINESS WAS NOT EXPANDING AS NO NEW SETTLERS were coming into the Battleford district to increase the volume of trade. In thinking over what could be done I considered the situation at Saskatoon which I knew was surrounded by excellent farming land ready for occupation. As soon as immigration started in this direction, these lands would be taken up. Up to this date the immigration authorities had been directing the incoming stream to Alberta along the Calgary and Edmonton Railroad. The land adjacent to the railroad was rapidly being settled and I was confident that before long there would be a movement in our direction. The remnant of the original Temperance Colonization Society settlers living near Saskatoon were getting into better shape since the Prince Albert line was opened and formed a basis for a certain amount of trade. Another factor that induced me to consider opening a branch in Saskatoon was that all my goods were shipped through that point and I had to pay forwarding and loading charges on all my shipments.

When it became known in Battleford that I contemplated opening a business in Saskatoon and possibly moving myself and family there, I was strongly advised against such folly. However their arguments were futile. I had waited patiently at Battleford for seventeen years.

The opening of railway communication had raised my hopes time and again but that desired consummation looked as far off as ever. The strongest factor of all was the advice of my worthy helpmate who urged me earnestly to make the venture. She declared her willingness to start roughing it again till we could afford to build a comfortable home. That meant much to me as it was going to strain my resources starting a new enterprise and made it undesirable that I should expend capital outside of my business. This willingness on her part was all the more commendable when it is kept in mind that we had a family of eight children and were leaving a commodious comfortable home in Battleford. Again I had to be thankful that I was blest with a considerate, helpful and brave companion in life.

It had got around that I was considering this undertaking and it reached Saskatoon. A firm there, James Leslie and James R. Wilson, upon hearing of it wrote offering to negotiate for the sale of the general store they were conducting. On the 5th of June 1899 I went to Saskatoon to investigate. It took just twenty minutes for us to make a deal. I bought the stock at a rate on the dollar and rented the building. On the 20th of the same month I returned to Saskatoon with one of my clerks to take stock preparatory to taking over the business. The store building was twenty-five feet frontage, going back about fifty feet and with a wooden shed at the back. It was built of stone boulders from the river, was plastered inside, and proved in winter to be very cold. The second floor was divided into rooms and had been occupied by the owners as a dwelling. The stock was not as large as I expected and was in dreadful shape. The former owners were not trained storekeepers and did not know how to take care of goods.

Saskatoon at this time consisted of a few houses on the east side of the river. The original settlement had been on that side but when the railway was built the station was placed on the west side of the river and a few buildings were erected. On the west side were the station house, the section man's house, the Mounted Police barracks, a stone building, a stopping house kept by the Kusch's, a hotel run by Don Garrison, and about six other houses and shacks. Soon after I arrived a building was commenced north of my store on First Avenue which was opened as a store by a Prince Albert firm, Bradshaw, I think the name was.

We set to work arranging our stock, cleaning out an accumulation of debris that had gathered into the corners, and getting into shape to do business as we thought it should be done. After a visit to Winnipeg and purchasing goods to complete the stock, it was found the premises were entirely too small to accommodate the stock and display it to advantage. I persuaded the owner to agree to build an addition of twenty-five frontage and the same depth back. This was done and ready for occupation by Christmas. The second floor of the new addition was used as a hall for some time.

In August 1899 there was a great flood on the North Saskatchewan River. I paid Battleford a visit whilst it was raging. On the trail approaching Battleford some of the bridges were afloat, the water having backed up in the creeks and carried them off the abutments. At Battleford the flats along the river were covered with water for the first time in my recollection. The old *North West*, a steamer belonging to the Hudson's Bay Company which had carried General Middleton's troops in 1885, broke away from its mooring at Edmonton and was wrecked on the piers of the bridge there.

On the 25th September I started with my family from Battleford for Saskatoon. We had a wagon with seats along the side which had been used a band wagon. I sat at the rear end to keep the children from falling out. We made the trip in two days, sleeping one night at the centre station. My wife laughed at herself as she had always maintained after her last overland trip from Swift Current that she would not move out of Battleford till she went in a Pullman car. Now, she said, "I had to go in a band wagon!"

I had arranged to board my family at Garrison's hotel, to which I took them but one month was enough for us. I need not dwell on the merits, or rather demerits, of this hostelry. Between incivility and inadequate and awful food it was simply abominable. One incident I will relate as illustrating the management of the house. I had been presented with a fine wild goose by one of the clerks who had shot it. I gave the goose to be cooked for our family. It happened to be train day (the train waited thirty minutes to let passengers have a meal) and a number of commercial travellers were aboard. So "mister man" dished up my goose to the passengers and my family got the bones! In remonstrating with the landlord I was told if I did not like it I knew what to do!

My wife asked to see the premises over the store. These comprised four small bedrooms, a small sitting room, and a smaller dining room, lighted by a sky light, and a kitchen. She at once decided to move into this miniature of a house. The bedroom occupied by my wife and myself (it was the largest) was large enough to accommodate a bedstead, a wash stand, and a bureau, leaving only enough space to enable one person at a time to dress or undress. You made your ablutions at the wash stand, turned round on your heels, and finished dressing before the bureau! When doing up the bedroom, the furniture had to be moved out first, into the sitting room, then replaced again. But my wife would endure anything rather than stay at the hotel. The following spring I rented the second floor of the new addition, making an entrance through the wall and dividing it up into three rooms, thus improving our accommodation.

The Doukhobors who had settled on the North Saskatchewan near Henrietta and at Red Berry Lake traded with us considerably. They were hard customers to do business with. When they first came in, having been accustomed to a style of bartering when buying, they never failed to say "too much" at the price asked and offered about half of what was the price. The consequence was that a great deal of time was wasted before the deal was finished. As they spoke very little English, it was hard to know what they wanted. Sign language was made use of profusely. One fellow made signs, first placing his two forefingers on his forehead, making motions as if milking a cow and then turning his arm around as if violently mixing something. He looked up appealingly and I suspected, correctly, that he wanted some butter! These people proved unsatisfactory settlers. They refused to conform to many of our laws relating to schools and marriage, and by refusing to become naturalized British subjects could not obtain patents for their homesteads. Many of them also were religious fanatics, at times starting on pilgrimages devoid of clothing which caused the authorities any amount of trouble. Living largely in community, their earnings were pooled. By living on the most frugal fare, entirely vegetarian, their leaders amassed large sums of money. When the final test came regarding their homesteads, the government refused them special privileges. Many then went to British Columbia and purchased land.

In 1900 Americans were coming to look over the lands. A few of us subscribed a fund to look after the people, taking them into the country to show them around. We gave them a welcome and tried to induce them to invest and our efforts had a fair amount of success. However, the numbers increased so rapidly we could not undertake entertaining all of them. The Canadian Pacific lands in the vicinity were being sold freely at two dollars and fifty cents per acre and the agents selling these lands attended to a lot of these prospective settlers. Lots in the town site began to move and a number were sold on building conditions. The price of lots at this date was thirty dollars each, half that price on condition of improvements being made to the value of two hundred dollars. I purchased three lots on First Avenue and as these were supposed to be a choice location I paid one hundred and twenty dollars for the three. I also purchased three on Second Avenue corresponding to the three on First Avenue for forty-five dollars for the seventy-five feet. I erected a grain warehouse and photographic studio as the necessary improvements and afterwards erected a large warehouse for storing goods. Freight began to come in freely and, accommodation in the freight shed being limited, I had to take immediate delivery of my Battleford shipments which I stored in this warehouse awaiting freighters from Battleford. I sold this property in 1906 for seven thousand, two hundred dollars, having no use for the warehouse after the CNR reached North Battleford.

Business was improving and with prospects of still further improvement I began to consider the availability of building a comfortable home for my family. After long consideration my wife selected the corner of Spadina Crescent and Nineteenth Street. The corner lot I purchased from the town site trustees for one hundred dollars was fifty feet by two hundred feet. The adjoining two lots I purchased from one of my clerks who had bought them intending to build a home but as his wife declined to stay in Saskatoon (they returned to Battleford) I paid him one hundred and fifty dollars for the two lots. This gave me a nice piece of ground two hundred and twenty-five feet on the crescent running back two hundred feet and not too expensive, five hundred dollars in all. In the absence of a local architect I procured a book of architects' sketches and selecting the style of house we fancied I proceeded to draw my own plans.

I let a contract for the labour, I supplying all the material, and had a commodious, comfortable home erected at a cost of six thousand dollars which we occupied for some years. In 1911, the government fancying the site for an armoury, bought the property from me for forty-seven thousand, five hundred dollars. Some buildings were being erected here and there in the town; the place was making a start.

The Governor-General, Lord Minto, paid Saskatoon a visit in the fall of 1901 and the usual address was presented. The school children, dressed in white, were at the station and sang "The Maple Leaf" as the train came in. The weather was stormy and falling snow made it necessary to have the address presented under cover. The only place available was my little store and into this the people crowded and the address was presented. At Prince Albert, where elaborate preparations had been made for His Excellency's reception, some misunderstanding occurred and no reception took place. Lord Minto did not even leave his rail car. The people there were very indignant at the slight handed out to that ambitious burg.

By this time Saskatoon had incorporated into a village. It was a hard struggle to count enough houses to effect this, the ordinance calling for twenty houses within a mile square. By counting all the shacks we managed it and at the date of the 1901 census we were credited with a population of 113. Great inconvenience was experienced having the post office on the east side of the river and so a petition was drawn up asking for a post office on the west side. This was granted and Allan Bowerman was appointed postmaster of West Saskatoon.

In the summer of 1902 the celebrated special train of American capitalists passed through Saskatoon. This excursion was organized by the Saskatchewan Valley Land Company. The party, gathered from various centres in the East, was brought from St. Paul, Minnesota, by this special train and was transported, dined and wined free to be shown a country awaiting development. I am credibly informed that so much land was sold that the whole cost of it to the Company was only fifteen cents per acre of the land sold during the trip. A great outcry was made in the Dominion Parliament regarding the deal made with the company but as far as we in this district were concerned, we owe largely to the company the rapidity of the settlement which ensued during the following three or four years. I for one do not grudge them the immense fortune they made out of the speculation.

We were quite delighted when Leonard Norman proposed starting a weekly newspaper in Saskatoon and gave him every encouragement. On the 17th October 1902 the first issue of the *Saskatoon Phoenix* was published. Amongst the advertisements in this issue appeared those of Young & Brown, general merchants; George Sillers, furniture; and Dr. P.D. Stewart, physician besides my own. It also contained a notice of the accidental death of W.H. Sinclair, legislative member for the district. He had gone out to shoot geese and, having got out of the wagon to shoot, when replacing the repeating shotgun in the wagon it discharged. The charge lodged in his breast, killing him instantly. His death was greatly regretted as he was a good businessman and seemed to have a great career before him. I felt it dreadfully as I had known him for many years and had been intimately associated with him from 1884 when he was in the Police force, which he left in 1889. After a short residence in Battleford he had come to Saskatoon and engaged in various enterprises.

The operation of the swing ferry was a great annoyance. An indignation meeting was held on the 24th October with Dr. J.H.C. Willoughby in the chair and Thomas Copland as secretary. It was resolved to approach the government to have the matter remedied. At the meeting it was stated "that the ferry was not run when the water was high, nor when it was low, nor when the wind was blowing and when these objections did not exist the ferryman was away doing some other job." I remember at this meeting the first suggestion to form a board of trade was made by Allan Bowerman.

A by-election to fill the vacancy created in the Legislature by the death of Sinclair was called for the 9th December 1902. B. Chubb had been in the field canvassing for some time but there was a decided feeling around Saskatoon against his candidature. A public meeting was held on the 22nd November to select a candidate. I was strongly urged to be a candidate but was very indifferent about doing so. However, I allowed my name to be put up with the others to a vote. The persons nominated at this meeting were Dr. Willoughby, Klassen (from Rosthern) and myself. Chubb would not allow his name to go to a ballot, saying he was going to run anyway and did not need any support from Saskatoon people. The ballot resulted in nineteen for Willoughby, five for Chubb (although his name was withdrawn) and fifty-nine for me. I accepted Chubb's challenge and proceeded to start my canvas. I found the most hearty response in and around Saskatoon and was confident of a large majority.

I went north amongst the Mennonites where Chubb expected to get support enough to offset the Saskatoon vote. I found that these people had been led to believe the contest was being run on Dominion political lines and they were decidedly hostile to my candidature, although very kind and hospitable toward me personally. At the town of Rosthern I could depend on a very few supporters. Affairs looked serious for me as I wended my way home. Two days before the election a few of my friends from Saskatoon went up to camp in the country till after the polling was over. The only hope was to induce as many as possible to ignore the election and refrain from voting on the plea that it was not a question of Dominion politics. The Mennonites as a rule, particularly the orthodox section, were indifferent to exercising their vote and on this forlorn hope we had to depend.

I had a little adventure on my trip through the Mennonite settlement. John Caswell agreed to drive me as he claimed to know the trails and some of the people. We drove through the Osler settlement and on to Hague, following the trail along the railroad. The snow was deep but the road being well travelled, the sleighing was good as far as Hague. From Hague we struck out west and northwest. In the afternoon we stopped at a house to get a meal and when we were ready to leave a snow storm with a high wind had started. Caswell was not very sure of the trail and before we made a couple of miles we floundered into a drift in which our horses were almost buried. The day was well advanced and darkness was coming on quickly. We decided it was taking chances to try to make it to the next house, about ten miles off, and turned back to the house we had just left to spend the night. The folks agreed to put us up for the night. The house was of boards, about sixteen feet by twenty-four feet, and one storey high with a shanty roof. It was banked high around with snow to keep out the cold. The family consisted of the man and his wife, one son about twenty, another about seventeen (who was an imbecile) and a daughter about twenty-two years old. The old man could speak a little English, the others none at all.

When bedtime arrived I wondered where we were to sleep. Preparations began by taking the table outside. Then a big mattress filled with feathers was placed on the floor. Another, similar, mattress was put on top of it and between the two we were to creep in and make ourselves comfortable. There were three bedsteads, one occupied by the man and his wife, one opposite to it by the girl and the two boys in another at the end of these. It was warm enough between the mattresses but, as these were filled with feathers direct from the fowl, when the heat from our bodies affected the feathers the odour was like sleeping in a hencoop. The old man had a bad cough and during the night he expectorated profusely, indifferent as to direction. I lay in constant dread of some disaster happening, being relieved only when I heard the plop on the floor. In the morning the storm had not abated and it was folly to think of travelling as the trail was entirely obliterated. We were compelled to stay in this shelter all day and another night. The hours dragged wearily. John and I ran out of subjects of conversation and the old man was unable to make us understand what he said. With only an old German newspaper to read and the poor imbecile lad every now and then peering into your face and giving you a kindly push with his hand, while laughing idiotically, affected my nerves. It was a relief when bedtime arrived.

Next morning the storm had ceased and we set out, ploughing our way through the drifts till we struck a main trail over which some sleighs had passed earlier in the day. That night we made Rosthern.

We were particularly anxious about the Hague poll. Marcotte, a French-Canadian formerly of Battleford and a fierce opponent of mine in my contest with B. Prince, was working for Chubb. He endeavoured to have a large body of foreigners around Fish Creek naturalized in time to vote and, if he succeeded in polling all of these for Chubb, my outlook was blue. Joe Fletcher, a staunch supporter of mine, offered to look after this poll. He challenged so many of the voters that the returning officer ran out of the printed forms of the affirmation early in the day. The poll clerk had to write out the form which took up so much time that when the hour of closing the poll arrived some of the voters could not get in the polling place. We had very grave doubts as to the validity of the naturalization papers these voters presented so my scrutineer was quite justified in objecting and causing their ballots to be reserved. The point was not decided in the courts because, even with counting these votes for Chubb at the final count, I had a clear majority.

At the close of the poll in Saskatoon I had a majority of seventy-five but the results from the outlying polls in the north were looked for anxiously. Robert Caswell, who was at the poll farthest from Rosthern, had arranged to send us the news but up to nine o'clock no word had come. The operator at Rosthern was about to close up his office when Caswell arrived and flashed the news. The number of votes was very small and, although strongly against me, the number was not sufficient to elect my opponent. We kept the news quiet. Chubb and his friends were confident of having been successful and were having a great celebration at the hotel. I called at the hotel and was the recipient of their sympathy in my defeat, for which I thanked them and joined with them in their rejoicing. Some of my friends, however, were so confident of my success that they freely accepted the wagers offered on all sides. Amongst my supporters, Jamie Flanagan was the most conspicuous. What a difference in the morning when the result of the northern polls was made public. As Flanagan said, "they had to take their medicine" but it was with considerable gagging.

At the final count by the returning officer, Don Garrison, some grave irregularities were disclosed in the northern polls. One deputy returning officer failed to put his initials on any of the ballots. At another poll the oaths to be taken by the officials were not recorded and at another the returning officer had put the key to the ballot box in the box before sealing it! The returning officer allowed all the votes to be counted as the election clerk and legal adviser considered them valid. Two of the polls should have been discarded. After all the votes were totalled, and allowing Chubb the thirty-eight challenged votes at Hague, I had a clear majority of fourteen. I was satisfied and did not call for a recount before a judge.

This fall J.F. Cairns came to Saskatoon to start in business and his first advertisement appeared in the *Saskatoon Phoenix* on the 5th December 1902. Soon after his arrival he called on me, presenting a letter of introduction from a mutual friend in Winnipeg. He told me his circumstances and of his intention to start a business in Saskatoon. I gave him every encouragement and told him of my faith in the prospects. Neither of us had any hope of the rapidity of the growth and development that subsequently took place but we were satisfied to take our chances of its becoming a place of importance and bent our energies to make it develop.

About this date the manager of the Imperial Bank at Rosthern, Mr. Hebblewhite, visited Saskatoon. I knew his father very well so he called on me and discussed the prospects for opening a branch of his bank at Saskatoon. Of course I pointed out the advantage of getting in on the ground floor in such a promising town. It was arranged between us that I was to let him know if I heard of any move on the part of any other chartered bank coming in. On the very train on which he travelled back to Rosthern, a representative of the Bank of Hamilton had arrived. I wired him this information and the next morning one of his men came in on the train, ready to open a branch of the Imperial. Too late—the Bank of Hamilton had hung out its shingle and started doing business.

In the summer of 1902 I met the Reverend Isaac M. Barr. He informed me of his scheme of founding a British colony west of Battleford and that he had obtained from the government the reservation of a large tract of land for that purpose. I paid little heed to his scheme as so many similar projects had come to nothing in the past. In November the papers began to give notice of his movements in England and it seemed as if something would come of it. From the cables appearing almost every day in the newspaper it was evident he was gathering together a formidable band of immigrants. He was a great believer in publicity, having all his movements recorded widely.

I wondered how he was going to transport his party, some two thousand people and all their belongings, the two hundred miles to the location of the proposed colony. I wrote him about this matter and he answered that he had made all the arrangements necessary. Connected with his scheme he professed to have organized a syndicate store, a transportation organization, a hospital, and other departments. A purchasing agent sent forward by Barr about the middle of January 1903 said he was authorized to purchase four hundred yoke of oxen, but when it came to the question of paying for these cattle he had no funds and so could do nothing. A brother, John Barr, a well-known, notorious character, procured some horses in the south country and loaded them in boxcars in such a manner that a great many of them smothered. When John Barr's cars came in he had no money to pay the freight on the consignment. He tried all around town to borrow money to release the cars and was very indignant at not being successful. In the meantime the several businessmen in Saskatoon were shaping themselves so as to be ready to furnish supplies for the crowd. I remember Cairns and myself, after a meeting of the Board of Trade, discussing the prospects. We decided to tax our resources to the limit in buying stock, determined to take advantage of the situation.

At eleven a.m. on Friday 17th April 1903 the first train came in, fourteen coaches with five hundred and ten people aboard. At six that evening a second train of eleven coaches with four hundred and ten people [reached Saskatoon] and on Saturday morning the third train arrived with five hundred and seventeen on board. The baggage followed in a few days on a special train of baggage cars. Barr had made absolutely no preparations to take care of this large body of men, women, and children. In London he had sold many of them, and been paid for, tents and waterproof sheets, guaranteeing to have them at Saskatoon awaiting their arrival. Some of the tents were in the baggage cars and some were never delivered at all.

The Dominion Immigration Department, anticipating trouble, had a large force of its men on the spot, under Superintendent Speers. These men provided some tents and endeavoured to alleviate the suffering as far as possible. After a few days the camp began to take shape. The weather was cold and bleak and the women and children, yes, and many of the men, unaccustomed to living outdoors suffered great hardship. A large number of the colonists were city-bred and entirely new to country life. They were almost helpless around a camp. Everyone was in good spirits and accepted the conditions for a short time without complaint.

As the days passed and Barr showed no disposition to help them to get started for their "land of promise," murmurs began to be heard. The mountain of baggage had not been sorted out, no attempt had been made to check it, and the poor folk could not get at their belongings. No sign appearing of the much vaunted supplies being available, business in the stores was flourishing. Cairns had a double shift of bakers turning out innumerable loaves that were carried off as fast as they came from the oven.

Ten days passed and the discontent was growing fierce. All kinds of threats were levelled at Barr who, arrogant coward that he was, slept in his tent with a revolver under his pillow. B. Prince and I went to Barr and made an offer to transport the whole party, bag and baggage, to their destination at a price per hundred pounds. We had our freight teams at Saskatoon waiting for our spring shipments and could have carried them off at once. Our offer was refused unless we agreed to give him a commission. As we made the offer through pity for the poor colonists, with whom we could deal directly and did not intend to make a cent out of the transaction, we refused his demand.

One morning I was presented with a petition signed by several hundred of the colonists asking me to address a mass meeting to discuss the situation. I asked Mr. Speers if I could use a large government tent to hold the meeting in and got his permission. A boy went round the camp with a bell calling them to assemble. When I reached the tent it was so packed with people I had great difficulty in making my way in. As soon as Barr caught sight of me he crowded through the surging mass toward me and demanded to know who gave me the right to use the tent. I told him Mr. Speers. He said it was his and not a government tent (which was untrue). He took hold of my coat, threatening to assault me. Mr. Copland and Mr. Leslie were right behind me. Two of the most peaceful citizens that ever drew breath had their hands raised to strike him when the Reverend G.E. Lloyd came between Barr and I. Soothing Barr with kind words, he advised me not to hold the meeting as there might be trouble. All this time not one of the malcontents who had requested me to come and speak to them made a sign of supporting me. I consented to withdraw as it was of no importance to me.

Several of the families dreading the long trek and subsequent isolation from railway facilities selected homesteads around Saskatoon. Many of those who had the means purchased horses and wagons and started out for themselves. Mr. Speers, upon seeing this, sent men ahead to put up signs at the branching trails to guide the travellers. They also erected large tents at intervals along the trail to serve as shelters. The excessive loads in some of the wagons was severe on the teams. They repeatedly were warned of the folly of loading so heavily but without much effect. Long before reaching their destination many of the teams became exhausted. I was sorry to see women trudging along the trail weary and footsore as I passed over the trail during the march.

Endless are the stories of the expedients some of them adopted to overcome the difficulties that cropped up. Afraid of losing their horses, some tied them to the wagon when camping, not allowing the poor beasts enough rope to graze and resulting in the loss of some splendid horses from sheer starvation. One outfit with oxen on descending a hill at Eagle Creek, thinking to prevent the oxen from going down too quickly, put hobbles on the oxen. Then when going up the hill on the other side of the creek, to prevent the wagon from slipping back, tied the wheels, making the oxen draw the load up the slope with the wheels locked. I have no desire to ridicule these unfortunate people who deserved to be commiserated with. Beguiled into conditions entirely strange and unused to prairie life, they struggled as best they knew to overcome the difficulties. Even after they got located on their homesteads there was great hardship and privation amongst them for some years. But now the district in which they settled is celebrated for the quality of grain produced. One family, Hill & Sons, have three times carried off the world's prize for oats at the Chicago exhibition, showing that the dogged resolution of the British spirit can overcome all obstacles.

Seeing the crowd flocking into the Battleford district, I was concerned about providing food for so many in excess of our usual population. The spring shipments had not gone forward and the supply of provisions was low. I went to Winnipeg, placed the situation before the CPR authorities, and arranged with them to forward a car of provisions and groceries with express speed. I had the car loaded Thursday and on

Sunday morning it was in Saskatoon. I had my freight teams waiting and early Monday they were on the trail. My wagons got into Battleford as the first of the colonists were arriving and the situation was saved.

All this suffering was the result of Barr's overpowering greed. The stupendous blunder was inducing people to settle in a district two hundred miles from a railway, especially a class of people unaccustomed to farm life. The florid pictures drawn by Barr of the preparations he had made for their welfare, promising them their own stores, their cooperative companies for tilling the land, the colony hospital, etc., were so alluring that he succeeded in beguiling many. Had Barr been satisfied with the usual commissions given for inducing immigrants he would have been well repaid, leaving others more experienced to cater to their wants. But no, he thought he could keep his hands on all the money his people had to expend and this excessive grasping made him lose all. By the end of May the colonists had deposed Barr from the leadership and replaced him with Reverend Lloyd. During the formative period of the colony, Lloyd proved a wonderful counsellor and a mountain of strength against discouragement. The next year a number more came out to settle in the colony. This time they took the railway to Edmonton and tried floating their effects down the river in scows, with disastrous results.

With Barr's party were a number of representatives of British newspaper syndicates. These correspondents chronicled every movement of the colonists, cabling long messages daily. These messages being published all over Britain, great interest was taken in Barr's "Britannia Colony." The name of Saskatoon was brought into prominence in British minds and placed it at once on the map as an important point in Saskatchewan. This publicity, at no cost to us, was a valuable factor in hastening the development of the town and the surrounding country. The citizens, realizing the foundation had been laid, built upon it through the Board of Trade's advertising campaign providing information relating to the district, with most gratifying results. These correspondents were a happy, genial lot of fellows. Those that followed the party to its destination amused us greatly in relating their experience of prairie travel. In such detail had the news been given that the escapade I had with Barr in the tent was cabled at great length. My friends in Scotland on reading it imagined I had been guilty of some terrible misbehaviour to be kicked out of Barr's tent.

Various business houses were being started, amongst them Isbister & Son in hardware, George Fraser in harness, Young in furniture, and Flanagan's hotel, all on Second Avenue. The *Saskatoon Phoenix* at the time carried an item claiming "The grading of Second Avenue will be a vast improvement. Now if we had a few loads of gravel placed on top, and a sidewalk laid." In June 1903 the southeast quarter of the school section adjoining the town was sold by auction. The portion on the west side brought one hundred and seven dollars an acre, thought to be an exorbitant price. Dr. Willoughby, the purchaser, had it surveyed into town lots and called it Riversdale.

The school district was divided and the portion on the west side was established as a district by itself. Soon after I came to Saskatoon I was elected to the school board. For some time the only school was the little stone school house [which was dismantled in 1911 and re-erected on the University of Saskatchewan campus]. All the children on the west side had to cross the river on the railway bridge, rather a dangerous walk for them. From the Temperance Colonization Company town site trustees we obtained a site on Third Avenue near Nineteenth Street and built on it the stone school latterly called the Pioneer School. Afterwards a frame building was erected alongside to accommodate the overflow of scholars.

Looking forward to the town extending north, the school board purchased the block between Twenty-Third and Twenty-Fourth Streets and Third and Fourth Avenues. The board had the temerity to pay seven hundred dollars for this block. As it was "out in the country," people were highly exercised over our extravagance and some called for our resignations. It can be imagined the consternation when we let a contract to R.W. Caswell at a price of thirteen thousand dollars for a brick school. Were we mad, burdening the district with such a debt? We kept our heads, telling them to wait and see. This block is now of immense value and so centrally located as to be talked of as a civic centre.

In July 1903 Saskatoon was incorporated as a town. Of the nine councillors nominated, only three were found to be qualified. The names of the others were not in the village assessment rolls of 1902, although some owned as much as $8,000.00 of recently acquired property. New nominations were held and the following were elected by acclamation: J.R. Wilson as mayor and T. Copland, J.A. Smith, W.R.C. Wallis, R. McIntosh, R.W. Dulmage, and Allan Bowerman as councillors. W.C. Sutherland was appointed secretary-treasurer.

During the winter of 1903–04 there had been a heavy snowfall and in the spring the thaw came rapidly, raising the river level even before the ice had become rotten. The ice began to move the 15th April, coming downstream in solid masses. The railway bridge, erected on wooden pile piers, failed to withstand the strain and first one pier then another gave way till four spans were in the river. The first span went out about nine-thirty in the morning and soon the cry spread, "the bridge is going down." Everyone deserted their work and hastened down to the riverbank. It was with sorrowful hearts we watched the other spans fall over. The ice, coming down in masses acres in size, tore the planking off the piers, snapping off the piles like pipestems. The chords, creaking and crashing, gradually fell over into the water leaving the rails held together by the fishplates, swaying in the air. When they touched the ice floes, they, too, were dragged down and disappeared. The sight was awe-inspiring with the mighty force of ice floes carrying destruction before them.

What of the effect on our town's rail communication, cut off for an indefinite period and just at the time when we were looking forward to trains of settlers arriving with their effects? The outlook was disheartening but worse news came over the wires. The valley at Lumsden was rapidly becoming flooded from melting snow and threatening to flood the railway track and prevent the trains from running. Twenty-four hours after the bridge went out, news came that the water was eight feet deep on the track and a mile wide. Bad enough that cars might be stalled on the east side of the river, it was a thousand times worse that they should be stranded at Regina. The Canadian Pacific Railway Company, realizing the seriousness of the situation, had train loads of material assembled on the mainline, awaiting the receding of the water at Lumsden, to have them rushed to Saskatoon. Three weeks passed before a train crossed the Qu'Appelle valley at Lumsden. Fortunately the train from Prince Albert going south had not gone through so we at least had intermittent service on the line north.

The commercial travellers gradually began to collect in Saskatoon (they had been scattered along the line on their spring trip) till over thirty of them were assembled. Full of life, they were driven to all sorts of expedients to pass the time. The first week passed pleasantly and then the idleness and uncertainty of relief began to tell on their spirits. The great fire in Toronto occurred at this time and we got meagre news telling of the destruction of many of their business houses, which caused a lot of them to feel blue. At last the flood receded at Lumsden and on the 20th May crossing there by boat was possible. The travellers, fitting up a boxcar with planks for seats, started off on a train from the east side for Regina. The CPR put an army of men to work erecting a temporary bridge and seven days from the time they started the trains were running over it. This was on the 3rd June, so for forty-nine days we were without train service. In the meantime an accumulation of settlers' cars had piled up at Regina and adjoining sidings. There were sixty-one cars of settlers' effects, three hundred head of stock, and nine hundred settlers. The stock had to be fed and the people lodged and fed at the expense of the railway company. A large number of settlers headed for our district were induced to go elsewhere along the mainline.

In September 1904 the third Session of the fifth Legislature was held. I pass over the previous two Sessions as nothing exciting occurred to ruffle the tranquillity of the Legislature. The demand for full provincial status was being urged strongly by the Territorial Assembly and executive council. Voluminous correspondence was carried on with the Dominion Government and a draft Bill was submitted by Haultain. The final letter from the prime minister, dated 30th September, intimated that should his government be sustained at the approaching General Election, negotiations would be entered into and a Bill granting provincial autonomy would be submitted at the next Session of Parliament. The House was prorogued on the 8th October and the Territorial Assembly became a thing of the past. This Session terminated my active participation in political affairs.

Looking back over the fourteen years I had served as representative in the Assembly, I am pleased to think that I had taken a part, however humble, in laying the foundation of and in helping to develop the great heritage in Western Canada. In the beginning the sparse settlement of the country, the lack of railway facilities, the great distances between settlements, and the lack of revenues made the task full of serious difficulties. The continued struggle with the Dominion Government for better terms, for fuller powers, and for greater responsibilities kept the mind in constant strain. It was with great satisfaction that I dropped out when our endeavour for full provincial autonomy was in sight. I rather liked the work of the Assembly but in connection with the position were other features that were distasteful to me. The having to plead for support at election times, the abuse you had to take from opponents (I fancy in my time I have been accused of every crime in the calendar, except bigamy), the misconstruction of your motives in your actions, the attention you have to give to trivial matters, and the impossible requests that are pressed on you by your constituents, I disliked and found burdensome.

By 1904 property was beginning to move lively. In the *Saskatoon Phoenix* of 13th May the following paragraph appeared:

> Saskatoon property is rapidly rising in value, and will doubtless soon reach high water, and bids fair to equal if not outstrip the price of our eastern cities. A deal was put through the other day, by which a piece of land on First Avenue changed hands at a price which worked out at exactly $5.00 per inch frontage.

A buoyant feeling was prevalent amongst the newcomers in the town. All were imbued with an optimism that Saskatoon was destined to become a centre. Newcomers in business were welcomed and encouraged and everyone pulled together to develop and boom the town. There were no petty jealousies of one another, in fact there was born what has become a classic expression—"the Saskatoon Spirit."

This summer saw great activity in the freighting of material from Saskatoon to the elbow of the North Saskatchewan River to build the Canadian Northern Railway bridge at that point. All the piles, timbers, cement, plant, and even coal for the engines were unloaded off cars at Saskatoon and taken in wagons to the bridge site. This gave employment to numerous teams, with many of the new settlers earning good money. The piles and timbers for the CNR bridge at Clark's Crossing were also unloaded at Saskatoon and floated down to the bridge site.

A movement of great import to Saskatoon was also started this summer. The population was increasing rapidly and the building of business places and houses was going apace. The optimism and unbounded faith in the future, with which we were imbued, impressed us with the necessity of laying the foundation of public utilities in the shape of a water supply and sewerage system. In order to lay out a comprehensive scheme, it was proposed that the villages of Riversdale and Nutana (which consisted of a small area on the east side of the river) should amalgamate with Saskatoon and seek incorporation as a city. In July 1904 a joint meeting of the Town of Saskatoon and the two villages was held and it was unanimously agreed to carry out the proposition.

In June 1906 the main line of the Canadian Northern Railway was completed as far as North Battleford. Construction trains were carrying passengers and I went up on the second train. The train going south passed Warman, or as it was then called, "The Diamond," early in the morning. When going from Saskatoon to North Battleford, to make this connection you had either to go up by rail the day before and stay over night or go by the road in the morning. The one hotel was conducted by my old friend Marcotte who was doing a roaring business. The trains north and south, east and west made no close connections so passengers were compelled to stay overnight. At this time the Prince Albert road was operated by the CPR which paid no attention to the schedule of the CNR, thus causing great inconvenience to the travelling public. The bustle attendant to the travel on the new line gave the people of the village of Warman exaggerated ideas of their position at the junction of the two railways. Two more large hotels were built and stores and lunch counters galore were started. Town lots were surveyed for a mile out and many sold at high prices. A map was prepared and displayed prominently which showed it as a great centre, with Saskatoon an insignificant point fourteen miles away. Alas, their high expectations were blasted when some two years later Canadian Northern bought the Prince Albert [Qu'Appelle Long Lake and Saskatchewan] and ran trains to suit the schedule of its main line. Passengers ceased to stop off and Warman became a deserted village; it even lost the name, "The Diamond."

The train arrived at North Battleford late in the evening. After applying and failing to find accommodation at the only house I could find on the town site, I wandered amongst the numerous tents and managed to get shelter with several others. The town site had just been laid out and numerous tents were pitched and several board shanties had been thrown together for the railroad men. The site was on the high land, about opposite Battleford, two miles from the river with rough slopes between. In the morning, after getting a rough meal, I got into a democrat to cross the river. When we arrived at the ferry, we found a long string of wagons and buggies waiting to cross. We waited for two hours before our turn came to go aboard. On the return journey my daughter, who had been visiting friends in Battleford, accompanied me. We left Battleford at two o'clock in the afternoon to insure our getting across the river that night. We reached the town site about sundown and no place could we find to stay the night. I hunted up the conductor of the construction train, a very courteous fellow called McKenzie, who, seeing our plight, gave us permission to use the smoking part of a composite car. He gave us some blankets and we fixed up beds, locked the doors and passed a comparatively comfortable night.

In September 1904 I had an architect in Winnipeg prepare plans for a large store on the corner of First Avenue and Twenty-First Street, the site I had purchased from Braithwaite. I intended to go on with the building in the following spring. Shortly afterwards I heard a rumour that the government was looking for a post office site as the original site selected and purchased had been condemned as too small. This property was on Second Avenue and was part of a site sold by J.F. Cairns that adjoined his store on the corner. I made an offer, which was accepted, of part of my property at the corner of First Avenue—one hundred feet on the avenue and ninety feet on the street, retaining fifty feet on the street for my own use. This was a good sale; I made seven thousand dollars and still had fifty feet frontage and one hundred feet in depth on which to build my own store.

There was a general desire expressed at a meeting of the citizens of Saskatoon that some measure be taken to obtain an outlet for the sub-surface water which underlay a portion of the town. In the construction of permanent buildings, it was found impossible to have satisfactory basements on account of this water. It was decided to put in a cellar drain from the corner of Twentieth Street and Second Avenue down the avenue to Nineteenth Street and then on to the river. For some reason, possibly financial, this was not completed till the water and sewer pipes were laid on this route. With regard to the proposed route of the Grand Trunk Pacific Railway, and the necessity of having it redirected through Saskatoon, at a meeting of the Board of Trade it was decided to send a delegation to Ottawa to press upon the government to have this done. The success of this pressure was announced in the *Saskatoon Phoenix* of 18th August 1905 as follows:

> The citizens of our town are naturally very jubilant over the authentic news from Ottawa that the main line of the G.T. Pacific was to pass through Saskatoon. Immediately on receipt of the news on Monday last a meeting of the Board of Trade was held and a delegation consisting of I.H. Lamont, M.P., Thos. Copland and F.R. Oliver was appointed to go to Montreal and Ottawa to make arrangements concerning the crossing and other matters in connection with the terminals. This was done at the request of Mr. Morse of the Grand Trunk Pacific Co. It is intimated that they may come on the present bridge and that a traffic bridge will be added. Saskatoon is to be the chief divisional point between Winnipeg and Edmonton and large shops are to be erected here and many men employed. As a divisional point for both the Canadian Pacific and the G.T.P. the citizens of Saskatoon have attained their highest ambition—that of being the most important town in Saskatchewan. This prominence will naturally lead to its selection as the capital of the province.

Following the formation of the two western provinces, Saskatchewan and Alberta, the location of the capital of Saskatchewan became a lively question. The claim of Saskatoon was brought to the front, its many advantages constantly being urged by its citizens. Each one having any influence was using their strongest endeavours to that end. A convention of boards of trade was held at Regina in July 1906 at which the whole convention was invited to visit Saskatoon. A special train was chartered by the Saskatoon citizenry and forty-eight delegates accepted the invitation. A banquet was tendered the visitors which was largely attended.

Everything went off swimmingly, the only discordant note being struck by a Regina man who, under the influence of John Barleycorn, made disparaging remarks against Saskatoon as compared with Regina which had been named the provisional capital in *The Autonomy Act*.

Just before the House met we compared notes and seemed to think we had a majority of the members pledged to support the claim of Saskatoon for the seat of government. I went to Regina along with a number of others to be present when the vote would be taken in the House. The evening before the vote I went to bed confidently advised that victory was ours. The morning of that eventful day it was rumoured that at a caucus held late at night the government had made it a party question and Regina was chosen. I went to the House to see it out. The motion that Saskatoon be selected was only seconded by the member for Rosthern in order to bring the matter before the House. Only two "aye" votes were recorded. I looked around at the members I knew had pledged their votes for us and thought of the slight regard some men had for their solemn promises. Back home we went, disappointed but not discouraged. Another important question had to be settled: the location of the University of Saskatchewan. We immediately braced ourselves for the fight and, as will be related further on, success crowned our efforts.

There had been considerable criticism of the town council during 1905 and much of it was unwarranted, as is usually the case. The tremendous optimism and enthusiasm caused people to expect more of the council than it could undertake with the slender means at its disposal and hence the desire for a more vigorous administration. The *Saskatoon Phoenix*, our only local paper, was strongly advocating M. Isbister for re-election as mayor. A section of the voters resented the proposition and strongly urged me to accept the nomination. I was indifferent as I had no particular fault to find with what had been done by the council with the means at its command. I recognized that under new conditions, when incorporation into a city had been accomplished (giving greater powers of borrowing), that more public improvements could be undertaken. Finally, after pressure was brought to bear, I agreed to allow my name to stand but I refused to take any means of furthering my candidature, either by personal canvas or public meetings. Nominations were made on

---

4th December, with the election to be held on the 11th. On Isbister's nomination papers were D.T. Smith, J.F. Cairns, B. Chubb, and W.A. Coulthard. On mine were J.D. Ferguson and F.A. Blain. The contest was keen with no politics being introduced, fortunately. The results gave Isbister 85 votes against 111 for me. Indication of the interest taken can be judged by the fact that every available vote but nine was polled, and these voters were absent from town. Even the lady voters came to mark their ballots. Isbister and I were in the polling station and were amused— as each lady passed out after handing in her vote, a smile was thrown in the direction of one or the other, giving us a slight indication of how she had voted. The *Saskatoon Phoenix*, writing of the election, said:

> From the hour of the nomination the contest was keen, and excited general interest to a greater extent than the contest between the candidates for the provincial representative. Both candidates got the support of many friends on the opposite side of politics, so that the result is without political significance. It was believed by many that Mr. Clinkskill was a strong and popular candidate. He had a clean record behind him after years in public life. Not one instance was ever quoted of his having done anything improper. His career in business was marked with success which stood him well in the absence of municipal experience in Saskatoon. He therefore enters upon his work as Mayor under most favorable circumstances. Saskatoon has an exceptionally bright future before it. It is for him to prove himself equal to the occasion.

Very fair words for an opposing paper, but its attitude changed in time when it feared I might become a factor in the political field. It might have saved itself the vituperations that were poured forth from time to time as my ambition in that direction was a negligible quantity.

The aldermen elected were J.R. Wilson, W.J. Bell, S.A. Clark, P.H. Currie, Harry Baker, and W.C. Sutherland (who resigned after being elected and Thomas Copland took his place). At one of the early meetings Dunning was appointed inspector, license inspector, and engineer of the fire engine! Dr. W.J. McKay was appointed medical health officer. We immediately started working on the proposed charter for the city. I took the Edmonton charter as a basis and, with a committee of three, had the draft prepared and passed by the council in March. The solicitor, D.T.

Smith, was unable to have it typewritten so the draft copy for presentation to the Legislature was written out in longhand! The Legislature passed the charter without any important amendments and on 1st July 1906 Saskatoon became a city.

The inauguration of the city was to take place on the 1st July and the town council was to cease on that date. Nominations for mayor and council were set for the 21st June when I was elected mayor and eight alderman were elected, all by acclamation. Only two of the old council consented to nomination. The city had by bylaw been divided into four wards, the alderman elected being for:

Ward One—R.B. Irvine and James H. Thompson
Ward Two—John Ashworth and William Hopkins
Ward Three—W.H. Coy and F.A. Blain
Ward Four—W.J. Bell and Thomas Copland.

The council and the people were impressed with a desire to own all our utilities. We had several offers to install electric power plants but all were rejected. The council engaged Wallis Chipman of Toronto to prepare plans for a system of sewerage, waterworks, and electric power. In April we let contracts for about one hundred and eighty thousand dollars to carry out the same. What a change in a few months. The former council hesitated about spending six thousand for drainage and now we committed the corporation for this seemingly huge sum. It was getting action on with a vengeance! The lowest bid on the contract for laying sewer and water pipe was so far below the next lowest bidder that the council hesitated about awarding it as it was less than half the next bid. Council decided to award it to the lowest bidder and was taught by this experience the folly of ignoring the qualifications and financial standing of the bidding party. After a time the contract was cancelled and the city proceeded with the work by day labour. A writer for Toronto's *The Globe* visited Saskatoon and on his return wrote to the *Saskatoon Phoenix* as follows:

> One's credulity is always being taxed to the uttermost regarding the reported triumphs and achievements of the west in these stirring days, but rarely more than when one stands in the streets of the thriving town of Saskatoon and is told that it was practically naked prairie four short years ago... . The town is moving with a swiftness that is phenomenal even for

the west. Old towns like Portage la Prairie and Prince Albert have waited a generation before installing a system of water-works and sewerage; in this Saskatoon is abreast of these and the numerous other towns of the west that are this summer introducing these prime factors in health and comfort.... At such a rate of speed one dare not make any prediction as to what Saskatoon will not have done by a generation from now.

A much respected citizen, Thomas Copland died on the 20th July 1906. He was called the "Father of Saskatoon," having come to the district as far back as 1882, and to him we were indebted for the fine, wide streets in the city. When surveyors were laying out the Temperance Colony town site, he insisted on the streets being laid out in the generous dimensions that we now enjoy. His passing away just as the fruition of his hopes for a great city were being matured was particularly saddening. Long will his memory be kept green in the hearts of the old-timers of Saskatoon.

A movement was started to build a hospital. A public meeting was held and a committee appointed to canvas for subscriptions and in a short time nine thousand dollars was subscribed. It was suggested that the city should aid by adding dollar to dollar to what was raised by public subscription. At a council meeting one evening I suggested to Dr. Munroe that if he made a motion that the city build a hospital as a municipal enterprise that I would support and advocate the proposition. On the 19th September Dr. Munroe's bylaw was passed by the council and was then submitted to the people. It passed with only seventeen votes being polled against the bylaw.

The Governor-General, Earl Grey, visited Saskatoon on 29 August 1906. Great preparations were made for his entertainment but owing to an accident which held him in Winnipeg (his eye had been injured by the bursting of an electric light bulb) the program could not be carried out. An address was presented at the station to which he replied before receiving a few citizens in his rail car while the Countess went for a drive around the city in an automobile. I got Hartley Chubb, who owned one of the few cars in Saskatoon at the time, to drive us. When we returned and left Lady Grey at the station, he started his car and before he had gone a few yards it came to a stop. His supply of gasoline had run out! I wondered what a pickle we would have been in if this had occurred when we were out a few miles. My wife and Lady Grey would have been compelled to walk back to the station.

It was decided by the council to procure a report regarding the possibility of developing power from the Saskatchewan River and C.H. Mitchell, a Toronto consulting engineer, was asked to prepare such a report on the proposed scheme. This report, received in July 1907, indicated that power could be obtained for 4300 horsepower at a cost of $6,970.00 and sold by the city at from $25.00 to $35.00 per horsepower. The report caused considerable comment amongst the citizens. It was recognized that one of the chief factors in attracting industries was cheap power and to achieve this objective the council was urged to proceed with the undertaking. The project hung fire, money stringency being one of the main reasons. At the next Session of the Dominion Government a syndicate of the citizens procured a charter for the scheme. In framing the charter the council succeeded in having the city's interests safeguarded in the event of it being considered advisable for the city to undertake the proposition.

Having purchased the Qu'Appelle Long Lake and Saskatchewan Railway on the 11th December 1906, the CNR gave the CPR notice to vacate the road by the 15th. There was a great hustle getting all its material and rolling stock gathered together and shipped out. At midnight on the 15th the whistles of the CPR locomotives sounded goodbye to Saskatoon for a time. It was just one year to the day till the first CPR train came in on its own line. Meanwhile, the Canadian Northern had not adequate rolling stock to properly operate the road it had purchased and for the ensuing months the service was most deplorable because the CNR was, at that time, our only railroad for getting in freight or passengers. To try and operate the road, old, superannuated locomotives had been bought and pressed into service. These played-out engines, fifty percent of their capacity at best, could pull only a small load and the severe weather made it difficult to keep up steam pressure. The engine drivers carried sacks of flour in the cab to use when the tubes started leaking! I have known of a train being stalled thirty miles out and three different engines being sent out to bring it in. When it did arrive, the greater part of the train was dead engines!

The winter was very severe, the scarcity of fuel was most acute, and caused great suffering—particularly in the country on farms distant from wood. In the city, stores were hard-pushed to keep their business places heated. Stocks of provisions fluctuated, sometimes running perilously low. My first visit in the morning was to the freight yards to see if any coal had arrived, sometimes getting a few hundred pounds at a time. At one time at the store we were compelled to burn lumber to get up enough steam to keep the building warm enough to prevent perishable goods from freezing. To add to the troubles of the railroad men, there were heavy snowstorms followed by strong winds that filled up the cuts on the line. Taken altogether, it was a very trying winter.

A fire destroyed the building occupied by *The Capital* newspaper on the 8th January 1907. The following day a public subscription was taken up, with contributors being from both political parties, and a handsome sum was presented to the publishers to enable them to start afresh. This is one instance of the wholehearted standing together of the Saskatoon citizens. Another of the same kind occurred about six months later when a large warehouse belonging to Cairns was burnt out. The bank he dealt with called his loan the following day and, on hearing this, a number of citizens offered him a loan to tide him over the crisis.

At the 1907 Session the Legislature passed *The University of Saskatchewan Act*. It provided for nine governors to carry on the business of the institution, three being appointed by the government, five elected by the senate, and the other member being the president, who was to be appointed by the governors. The governors were A.F. Angus, Levi Thompson, John Dixon, Arthur Hitchcock, James McKay, A. MacDonald, A.P. McNab, and myself. The board met at Regina and elected Angus of Regina as chairman. Three of the members went East to engage a president for the university. After their return, at a meeting held on 20th August 1908, W.C. Murray of Dalhousie University was appointed to the position.

The first step taken by the governors was to decide the basis on which the university was to be organized. In order to get all information possible of the experience of similar institutions, a delegation was sent to the East and to the United States. From a report made by this delegation, the governors decided to recommend to the government that the university should embrace in its operation an agricultural college. Recognizing that the industry of the province was essentially of an agricultural nature, emphasis was laid on this aspect. Reports from some institutions recommended that the location of the university should be adjacent to the political capital, which opinion did not quite fit in with the ideas of some of the governors—those from the North, particularly.

Having decided on the scope and aims of the institution, the next business taken up was the location. The board was invited to visit several cities and towns aspiring to be the location of the university. Moose Jaw, Prince Albert, Battleford, Qu'Appelle, Regina, and Saskatoon all were visited and the advantages of each were laid before the members of the board. On the fifth of April the board met in Regina and amongst other business transacted was the selection of the location. I may mention that McNab, having been taken into the government, resigned his seat on the board and W.J. Bell was appointed in his stead. On the 7th April 1909 we were shown around Regina and the proposed site was pointed out. It afterwards transpired that the larger portion of the land shown to us belonged to the government, although the Regina people had led us to believe it was to be donated by them. Battleford offered a site of one thousand acres free and Frank Cahill of Saskatoon offered a choice of one thousand acres out of a large tract as a donation.

When the order of business at our meeting reached the question of location, the nerves of all the members were in a state of high tension. Each member voiced his opinion and set out the advantages of the location he favoured. Before going to this meeting Bell and I had a meeting in Saskatoon with several prominent citizens and we were empowered by them in writing to guarantee that a site suitable and satisfactory to the board would be procured at a cost not exceeding one hundred dollars per acre and of at least one thousand acres in extent adjacent to the city. This was used by Bell and I as a trump card. When the balloting commenced the tension was so acute that I could hear the hearts of the men on either side of me throbbing! We first cast an open ballot for the different places. Then, in succeeding ballots the lowest was discarded till it fined down to Regina and Saskatoon. When this ballot was taken there was a silence in the room that could be felt. After the decision we mutually agreed that the actual figures should not be made public. Sufficient to say that Saskatoon was the choice. If the figures had been divulged, there would have been on the part of the public all sorts of surmises as to how this member and that member had voted. The reaction after the intense excitement left Bell and I in a state of collapse—we felt like wet rags. Wandering down to the telegraph office, we flashed the news to Saskatoon. On going to the hotel we were surprised to find no one about. It was evident that the people were so confident that Regina would be chosen as the location for the university that no interest was evidenced on their part. We hunted around to find McNab who was keen to know the result and then went to bed. Next morning we took the train for home.

When the train reached Dundurn a special car from Saskatoon, filled with a joyous crowd of our fellow citizens whose rapture at our success was unbounded, was hitched onto our train. On arriving at Saskatoon everyone and his wife and all the kiddies were at the station to welcome us. The steam whistles were blowing and bells ringing and the cheers and hurrahs sounded till throats were sore. I managed to slip away in the crowd and went down to my home. Soon a happy procession appeared headed by a band. A buggy drawn by ropes and containing the mayor, McNab, and Bell followed. I was hustled into a rig and the procession proceeded uptown to the corner of Second Avenue and Twenty-First Street where a halt was made and speeches demanded. When the news reached Saskatoon the night before, about eleven-thirty, it soon spread. Whistles sounded alarming the whole town. People got up out of bed to ascertain the reason for the noise and on finding out what it was about got into the streets in crowds. The rejoicing was kept up for a couple of days, winding up in a torchlight procession.

The board met at Saskatoon on the 29th April 1909 and selected a site on the east side of the river, just opposite the public park, for the university. We obtained eleven hundred and seventy-six acres at a cost of slightly under one hundred dollars an acre. We afterwards purchased another quarter section at a cost of eighteen thousand dollars. After investigation we appointed as our architects the Montreal firm of Brown and Vallance and on the 25th June 1909 instructed them to prepare plans for the construction of five buildings, including the powerhouse from which we intended to furnish steam for heating all the buildings by conveying the steam pipes and electric wires in a concrete tunnel underground. The buildings planned were an academic or teaching building, a residence for one hundred and twenty-five students, a stock pavilion, an engineering building, and the powerhouse.[1]

By early 1907 the depression in financial affairs was affecting everyone. Money was scarce and business was slow. No one, however, was discouraged but looked forward to a recovery. The city itself was up against it for money. The debentures for the new works had not been sold and, the bank having refused further advances, great difficulty was found in even paying officials' salaries. Mayor Wilson pledged his own private funds to the extent of $40,000.00 to help out the city. Before relief came by selling bonds, an electrical firm which had supplied some machinery threatened to seize the power plant. The mayor went around and raised sufficient funds from a few citizens to pay off this account—another instance of "the Saskatoon Spirit"!

In July 1907 the Canadian Northern made known its intention of building a line through the Goose Lake country to Calgary, to enlarge the roundhouse and shops, and to build a new passenger depot opposite Twenty-First Street. This last move suited me alright as it enhanced the value of my store property. Also during this year the post office and courthouse were started on Twenty-First Street. The foundations for the post office were completed before winter set in and in the fall of 1908 the building itself was finished.

In February 1908 I decided to sell out my Battleford business. The running of two large businesses proved too great a strain on my resources

---

1. The board subsequently purchased an adjoining piece of land of about 380 acres. Of the site, 293 acres (with a frontage on the river of half a mile) was set apart for the campus, 361 acres for experimental plots, and 915 acres for the farm. The board had the architects prepare a comprehensive plan for the campus, showing the location of the different buildings as they may be erected. The first structures were to be erected on the eastern boundary, away from the river, with future buildings to be constructed towards the river.

so I sold off the stock. The next year I closed up the department store in Saskatoon and divided the premises into stores with offices above, retaining one store for a clothing and shoe business. I was determined to take life easier after the strenuous years I had spent in business. Accordingly, on the 9th September 1908 I started on a trip to Scotland accompanied by my wife and son, James Thomas, or "Tom." In contemplating this trip it at first was intended that only my son would go with me. Late the evening before our departure we persuaded my wife to accompany us and in the morning she packed up and was ready to go with us! We returned home in December, just before Christmas. Whilst I was in Glasgow I endeavoured to sell the Saskatoon debentures but found that this class of bonds were not popular, the repayment being in annual installments. Those running for a long term, providing interest semi-annually, and with a sinking fund to pay them off at maturity were most in demand. I finally made a contract with a firm to buy them at 90% but the firm failed to carry out the agreement. This was a great disappointment to me as I had spent a great deal of time negotiating with different parties. It practically spoiled the pleasure of my trip.

Heavy rains in the southern part of Alberta caused a great rise in the river which rose to within four inches of the record height. In June 1908 some men from Medicine Hat attempted to take a steamer named after their town to Grand Rapids. They got as far as Saskatoon and passed under the railway safely when something went wrong with the steering gear. It became unmanageable and was dashed against the traffic bridge, which carried away the upper works. The current then swung the boat round on one of the concrete piers. We viewed the accident from the window of our home. The excitement was intense as we could see the men on board climbing onto the bridge. The engineer, who lingered to let off the steam, fearing an explosion, jumped into the water and landed a short distance downstream. A barge containing coal, which was lodged alongside the steamer, was cut loose to lighten the strain as they tried to pull the steamer off the pier. As soon as the barge was released, the steamer slowly keeled over and sank. The owners lost the vessel and the cargo, the only salvage being the machinery and some of the upper timbers.

Early in January 1909 James Flanagan died. He came to Saskatoon when it was a very small place and helped largely in its development. He was very popular and was a great booster of real estate prices, believing strongly in the future of Second Avenue as a retail business street. His manner was brusque, forming strong friendships and equally strong dislikes. Shortly after his arrival he asked me to purchase some home-cured bacon he had brought with him from Oak Lake where he formerly kept a hotel. It was peculiar looking stuff, being cut in small pieces and covered with dark spots as if it had been rolled in the dust. I took a chance on it, giving him the price he asked. This trifling incident seemed to have pleased him so much that afterwards, when furnishing the Western Hotel and the Flanagan Hotel, he gave me extensive orders for dry goods, cutlery, etc. These ventures strained his resources and he was a long time paying for his purchases. He was very touchy about debt so I gave instructions that my accountant was not to dun him. Every few weeks I would casually drop into the hotel and when I happened to encounter him he would write out a cheque, thrusting it into my hand and in a humorous way ordering me out of the house! His peculiarities were the subject of endless stories. For instance, he said he made it a rule never to take a drink alone but in the event of no one being around he would, after pouring out a portion, drink to his own reflection in the mirror!

The year 1909 closed with prospects brightening. The money stringency was beginning slowly to pass away. There was a good wheat crop averaging twenty-one bushels per acre for the province and the price was fairly good. The new year of 1910 opened with everyone feeling hopeful. The city council outlined expenditures in public improvements aggregating two hundred thousand dollars. In April the university's board of governors let the contract for buildings costing about six hundred thousand dollars. The outlook for employment of labour was bright as many private buildings were projected in addition to city and university works. On the 4th of May the first sod of the university work was turned by Chancellor E.L. Wetmore without much ceremony.

Prime Minister Sir Wilfrid Laurier visited Saskatoon and was given a civic reception. The city was decorated with arches being erected at different points. It was certainly a wholehearted welcome to the distinguished statesman. Sir Wilfrid also laid the cornerstone at the university and of Saint Paul's church. During the ceremony at the university a fine view from there was obtained of a spectacular fire on the west side where the tanks and warehouses of the Winnipeg Oil Company were destroyed.

That Saskatoon was becoming noted as a distributing centre was well evidenced by the number of large warehouses being erected by wholesale firms during 1910. Implement houses and grocery and hardware firms had erected or were in the course of constructing large, substantial premises. The total building permits issued were of a value of $2,817,771.00. The city was on the eve of the greatest expansion in its history. Real estate was advancing in price and showed great activity.

The board of governors of the university decided, in order to expedite business and to lessen the necessity of calling the full board together, to appoint an executive resident or nearby resident to Saskatoon to which was delegated power to carry on the day-to-day business, with the full board meeting occasionally to confirm appointments, pass estimates, decide on questions of policy, etc. Consequently W.J. Bell, President Murray, and I, with the two members from Prince Albert to be called on when necessary, were appointed to this executive. I was elected chairman of the board in place of A.F. Angus of Regina who had resigned.

This university was starting out under the most favourable auspices. There was no hampering of the governors with religious entanglements. We were willing and anxious that theological colleges should be founded and affiliated with the university. We prepared to allocate sites for their buildings with the only condition being that the architecture should be the collegiate Gothic adopted by the university. It was entirely free from political influence, although a provincial institution and supported from provincial revenues. The choice of Murray as president was a very fortunate one:, he is a man of high character, a good academic scholar, a great organizer, and a most indefatigable worker.

When the civic elections were held in December 1910 I was induced to become a candidate for mayor. I was elected by a nine-three majority, my opponent being Robert McIntosh. Under a bylaw passed by the council of 1910, the mayor was ex-officio one of the commissioners. I recognized that there was a demand on the part of the citizens for a more active policy in the matter of development of public improvements and utilities. The council elected, being largely new men, were imbued with the same desire. My anticipations as to the responsibility of the commissioners acting as managers of the civic business was short-lived. Some of the aldermen who were opposed to the commission form of government succeeded in having the bylaw amended by striking out the provision of a two-thirds majority being required to reject a report of the commissioners, thereby limiting the responsibility of that body and insisting on certain business being laid out before some of the former committees before being submitted to the council. To my mind this was taking out the keystone of the fabric of the commission form of government and reverting to the former system of committees of the council. However, I endeavoured to carry out the work as well as I could under the circumstances.

The importance of improving the quality of the water pumped from the river had been under consideration by the former council and the engineer was instructed, while on his vacation, to inspect various filtration plants and to report. The result of his inspection was embodied in a report recommending a system of mechanical filtration as designed by the Roberts Company of Philadelphia. In calling for tenders for a water filtration plant, a proposition was submitted by an English firm for a system of filtration by pressure. This system did not appeal to me as suitable for the very turbid water we had to contend with at certain seasons of the year and I opposed it very strongly. Eventually the council accepted the Roberts system which has proved a most unqualified success. The water now is pure and sparkling and by using a small quantity of alum as a coagulant we obtain practically sterile water.

The condition of the old power plant was inadequate for the demand for light and power. The powerhouse erected in 1906, designed to supply a population of fifteen thousand people, was too small to admit of any more machinery being installed. The question before us was either an extension of the present building or an entirely new building on another site. The disadvantage of the old site was the lack of trackage for bringing in fuel. When this site was selected by the council of 1906, part of the scheme as outlined by Wallis Chipman was an aerial tramway from the other side of the river to connect with the railway, but this tramway had not been installed. The commissioners recommended that a new site be purchased and a building erected capable of providing for future need as well as present demand. We could foresee a large, increased demand owing to the expansion of the city. In selecting the site we had to keep in view the necessity of easy access by railroad track, a central location for distribution of electricity as well as keeping in view the possibility of someday using the exhaust steam for heating purposes and getting sufficient area to allow of extending the building as well as space for storage of coal to forestall a possible shortage through strikes or inclemency in winter causing a tie-up on the railways.

We selected a site on Spadina Crescent on the river bank between Avenues A and B and recommended same to the council for approval. To prevent any proprietor of the lots holding us up in the price, we had taken the precaution of obtaining options on the property through outside parties before making our report. This proved to be a wise step as one of the owners was particularly wroth at the commissioners. He declared we had defrauded him of a large sum by keeping back the information that the city was purchasing the property! The commissioners, along with the architect, designed a building to hold machinery and boilers capable of generating four thousand horsepower, with sufficient land to double the building.

One mistake was made and that was installing a reciprocating engine of seven hundred and fifty kilowatts. We ought to have purchased a turbine as this machine is much more economical in operating. There was no error made regarding boiler equipment. Babcock and Wilcox boilers with automatic chain grates, overhead bunkers and coal elevating machinery, economisers, and every known device for economical operation were purchased. Whilst this plant was being manufactured we had a strenuous time supplying the increasing demand for electricity. The old plant was working continuously on an overload of fifty percent of capacity. Many an anxious night I spent fearing a breakdown in the plant. We did have a stoppage in the summer when some tubes in one of the old boilers collapsed and two men were severely injured by scalding steam. This was a very serious matter as it affected our water pumping machinery as well. However, in forty-eight hours the steam was on again, much to my relief.

The years 1911–12 witnessed the greatest development of public improvements in the history of the city—miles of concrete sidewalk, street paving (asphalt and bitulithic), water mains and sewers, an intercepting sewer to a sewage disposal plant, fire halls, firefighting equipment and hospital accommodation were constructed and purchased. The erection of business blocks, warehouses, and residences went on apace with several million dollars being invested in this way. The city limits were enlarged taking in a number of new subdivisions and the assessment went up by leaps—in 1912 it was $36,897,498.00, an increase over 1910 of over twenty-six million dollars. Building permits for 1911 were $5,208,366.00 and $7,640,530.00 for 1912.

In 1911 the council made an agreement with a syndicate to develop water power from the river. In consideration of carrying out the undertaking, it was given a franchise for a street railway within the city limits. The engineers employed by the syndicate, after a thorough investigation into the whole scheme, reported that the cost would be largely in excess of the original estimate and that the power available from the river flow was so limited that it was not a feasible proposition from an economic standpoint. The syndicate asked to be released from the agreement and this was acceded to by council. With the consent of the people, the council constructed the street railway as a municipal enterprise.

In the midst of all this mighty onrush the city council and commissioners had a busy time dealing with the problems presented for solution. The ordinary run of citizens do not realize how much they are indebted to the men around the council board for their singleness of purpose and devotion to duty. It is a great satisfaction to me to testify that during these strenuous years there never was the slightest desire evidenced by any one of the members to influence the decision of the council to their individual benefit. It was not all a bed of roses for the occupant of the chair and on one occasion they, in their wisdom, thought fit to censure him for having made remarks derogatory to their dignity which unfortunately were reported in a newspaper. However, the motion was rescinded at the next meeting of council. At the end of my second year, in 1912, I take pride in recording that my colleagues on the council favoured me with their appreciation of my leadership by presenting me with a gold watch and from the heads of the departments, a silver loving cup.

Postscript

THE PERIOD COVERED BY THE FOREGOING NARRATIVE has seen Western Canada develop from a "Great Lone Land" into a vast stretch of cultivated fields with room for millions of settlers (only one-fifth of the land fit for cultivation has been turned by the plough); from a country devoid of railway communication to one rapidly becoming a gridiron of steel tracks; from a territory governed by appointees of the Federal Government to provinces with full powers of government. Whilst the development of the agricultural possibilities of the soil has been demonstrated by the production of millions of bushels of grain, the industry is but in its infant stage. When diversified farming and more intensive cultivation (which is being advocated and encouraged by the Dominion and Provincial Governments and the great corporations whose interests are identified with the country) has become general amongst the farmers, the potential of the land will begin to be evidenced. In a very short time I look for Western Canada not only to be able to feed the British people with all the cereals they can consume but also to supply the local demand for meats taking the place of the foreign supplies that are now drawn on so largely.

The incoming settler of today finds a very different condition of affairs in contrast with that of the immigrant of the latter part of the last century. Then he went on his land and commenced operations entirely in the dark as to the methods. Now there is all sorts of information supplied by the government for the asking. Experimental farms demonstrating various methods for cultivating different kinds of grain have the results of years of operation available for the farmer. The provincial college of agriculture sends lecturers to all the little towns and villages who talk directly to the farmer on all subjects connected with grain raising, stock breeding, dairying, poultry raising and even domestic science. The government has, by aiding co-operative elevator companies, improved the marketing of grain and has established a commission that attends to all complaints regarding shipping and forwarding of the products. Some of the large land corporations will provide ready-made farms to enable a farmer to commence making a living immediately. The government will even supply stock on long-term payments to any bona fide farmer who wishes to start cattle breeding. Apart from agriculture, the mineral, timber, and fishery resources are yet to be tapped.

In concluding this simple tale of arduous, strenuous pioneering in the greatest of all the British colonies, I wish to say that if I have succeeded in interesting the reader my efforts shall have been amply repaid.

Index

A
Alberta district (school), 83
Albion Hotel, 90
American capitalists, 130
Angus, A.F., 152, 158
Ashworth, John, 149
Assiniboia district (school), 83
Athabasca Landing, 118
Autonomy Act, The, 147

B
Babcock and Wilcox boilers, 160
Bad Arrow, 67
Badger House, 121–22
Baker, Harry, 148
Bank of Hamilton, 135
Bank of Montreal, 119
Barr, John, 136
Barr, Reverend Isaac M., 135–37, 139–40
Bartering, 128
Batoche, 19, 26, 31, 33, 59–60, 96
Battle River, 23–24, 27, 34, 36, 39, 41–42, 46, 53, 55, 60
Battleford (1882–1885), 20, 23–24, 26–29, 33–34, 44–45, 52, 59, 61
Battleford (1886–1899), 67–68, 70, 73–74, 81–83, 86, 93, 95–99, 103, 109–10, 112, 114–15, 117, 120–21, 123
Battleford (1900–1912), 125–27, 129, 131, 133, 135, 139, 145, 153, 155
Battleford district, 124–25, 138
Battleford Rifles, 31, 34, 53
Beaver River, 52
Bell, W.J., 148–49, 153–54, 158
Bernier, Mr., 73
Berthiaume, Mr., 34
Betts, J.R., 84, 99, 102
Big Bear, 28, 45, 47, 61
Bird, Jim, 30, 49
Blackfoot Crossing, 68
Blackfoot Indians, 68
Blain, F.A., 148–49
Board of Trade, 131, 136, 139, 146
Bouchier, Mr., 97

Bourinot, Mr., 111
Bowerman, Allan, 130–31, 141
Bradshaw (a firm), 126
Braithwaite, Mr., 145
Brandon, 4, 6–7
Bresaylor settlement, 33, 40, 46, 69, 78, 81, 108–9
Brett, Dr. R.G., 81, 84–85, 88–89
Britannia Colony, 139
British North America Act, The, 79
Brown and Vallance, 155
Buffalo, 21, 70–71, 88, 97, 120
Buffalo Head, 120
Bulyea, G.H.V., 122–23
Burke, Paddy, 54, 56

C
Cahill, Frank, 153
Cairns, J.F., 135–37, 145, 148, 152
Cameron, M.C., 123
Campbell, Daniel, 102
Canadian National Railway, 129, 143, 151
Canadian Northern Railway, 144, 155
Canadian Pacific hotel, 3
Canadian Pacific Railway 6, 15–16, 25, 49, 129, 138, 141–42, 144, 146, 151
  Mackenzie survey, 83
Capital, The, 152
Carlton, 24, 26, 34, 48
Caswell, John, 132, 134
Caswell, R.W., 140
Cayley, Mr., 83, 84, 89, 95, 99–101
Cedar Lake, 17
Census (1901), 130
Chipewyan Indians, 122
Chubb, B., 131–34, 148
Chubb, Hartley, 150
Clark, S.A., 148
Clark's Crossing, 143
Clink, D.L., 76, 78
Clinkskill, Dora (daughter), 66
Clinkskill, Dora (wife), 26–27, 31, 35–37, 39–40, 42–43, 47, 54–55, 57–59, 66–67, 92–93, 98, 125–29, 151, 156

Clinkskill, James, 89, 94, 106, 148
Clinkskill, James Thomas (son), 156
Coal mines, 114
Coal oil, 20, 52, 54
Cochin, Father, 61
Cold Lake, 122
Commercial Bank, 16
Company School of Infantry, 54, 56
Copland, Thomas, 131, 137, 141, 146, 148–49
Father of Saskatoon, 150
Coulthard, W.A., 148
Council of Public Instruction, 106–7
Cowan, Constable, 51
Coy, W.H., 149
Craig, Mr., 114
Crooked Leg, 67
Crozier, Superintendent, 34
Crystal City, 5–6
Cumberland House, 18, 22
Currie, P.H., 148
Cut Knife Creek fight, 56

D
Dalhousie University, 152
Daunais, C.M., 117–18
Davidson, Mr., 89
Davis, Joe, 116–17
Davis, T.O. (Tom), 17, 115–16
Dawson, 118–9, 122
Delaney, John, 45
Delaney, Mrs. John, 45
Devil's Gulch, The, 72
Devil's Lake, 70
Dewan, Tom, 39, 109, 115, 117–18, 120–22
Dewdney, Edgar, 82
Dickens, Inspector, 45, 51–52
Dill, George, 45, 65, 67
Dixon, John, 152
Doukhobors, 128
Duck Lake, 25–26, 31, 35, 58
Dulmage, R.W., 141
Dundurn, 154
Dunning, Mr., 148

E
Eagle Creek, 27, 30, 72, 87, 138
Eagle Hills, 31, 41, 46, 59, 91
Edmonton charter, 148

Election (1887), 68–70, 78
Election (1891), 91–92, 96, 99, 101, 107–8, 111
Election (1896), 114, 116–17
Electric power plants, 149, 155, 159
Emerson, 4–6

F
Fafard, Father, 45, 67
Farming, 12, 15, 33, 68
Federal grants, 86
Ferguson, J.D., 148
Fish Creek, 133
Flanagan Hotel, 157
Flanagan, Jamie, 134, 140, 157
Flat Creek, 7, 14–15
Fletcher, Joe, 133
Forget, A.E., 26, 79, 106, 109, 116
Fort Pitt, 41, 44, 46–47, 49–52, 92, 104, 109, 119
Fort Saskatchewan, 119
Foulkes, Mr., 56
Fraser, George, 140
Freeman, Barney (or Freemont), 39, 60
Frog Lake, 27, 41, 44–45, 65
Frog Lake massacre, 46, 119

G
Garrison, Don, 126, 134
Garrison's hotel, 127
Gilchrist, William C., 45
Gisborne, Superintendent, 87
Globe, The, 149
God Save The Queen, 79
Gold, panning for, 104–5
Goose Lake country, 155
Gopher Creek, 8, 14
Gopsil, George, 38–39
Gordon & Ironside, 122
Gordon, J.T., 104
Goshen, 88
Gouin, Charles, 67
Govin, Charles, 45
Gowanlock, John C., 45
Gowanlock, Mrs. John C., 45
Grand Rapids, 16–17, 156
Grand Trunk Pacific Railway, 146
Great North West Central Railway, 82–83
Grey, Earl, 150

Grey, Lady, 150–51
Grizzly Bear's Head Reserve, 41

H
Hague, 132, 134
Half-breed claims, 81
Half-breed runners, 28
Half-breed scrip (certificate), 4
Half-breed settlements, 31, 44, 69
Half-breed woman, 66
Half-breeds, 24–25, 27, 30, 48, 71, 82,
    91–92, 98, 121
    digging Seneca root, 113
    land titles of, 21
    members of Assembly, 96–97
    rebellion of, 20–22, 59–61
    requesting meeting with Indian Agent,
    36
    selling buffalo bones, 88
Half-breeds, French, 40, 69
Half-breeds, hostile, 33, 49, 70
Half-breeds, Scotch, 40
Half-breeds, trusty, 35, 39, 46
Haultain, F.W.G., 80–81, 83, 89, 95, 99–92,
    110–13, 142
Hebblewhite, Mr., 135
Henrietta, 114, 128
Heon, Joe, 49
Herchmer, Colonel, 44, 49, 53
Hill & Sons, 138
Hitchcock, Arthur, 152
Hodson, Robert, 67
Hodson, Tom, 38, 52
Hoey, Mr., 88
Home Guards, 31, 38, 54–55, 58
Homesteading, 6, 33, 122, 128, 138
Hoodoo, 26
Hopkins, William, 149
Hourie, Peter, 60
Hudson's Bay Company, 3, 21, 36–37, 45,
    54, 88, 127
Hudson's Bay Company steamer, 16–17
Hudson's Bay factor, 34, 44, 51
Humboldt, 26, 44

I
Immigration, 125, 135, 139
Immigration Department, Dominion, 136
Imperial Bank, 135

Indian Agent, 28–29, 34, 36–37, 45, 58,
    110, 117
Indian reserves, 27–28, 41, 74
Indians, 29, 31, 33, 38, 41, 46, 98, 114
    guilty, trial of, 67
    hostility of, 35–37, 46, 48, 50–55, 57, 59,
    61
    land of, 111–12
    voting by, 78
Insinger, F.R., 101
Iron Body, 67
Irvine, R.B., 149
Isbister, M., 147–48
Isbister & Son, 140

J
Jackfish Lake, 98, 114
Jackson, Gid, 118
Jackson, William Henry (or Honoré J.
    Jaxon), 21
Jarvie, Baillie Nicol, 114
Jelly, D.F., 84
Journals of the Legislative Assembly of the
    North-West Territories Council, 100

K
Klassen, Mr., 131
Klondike gold rush, 118–19
Kusch's (stopping house), 126

L
Lac la Biche, 46, 123
Laird, D., 69
Lamont, I.H., 146
Latour, W., 117
Laurie, P.G., 23, 76
Laurier, Sir Wilfrid, 114–16, 157
Leduc, Father, 106
Leeson & Scott, 120
Leslie, James, 126, 137
Liquor, 26, 31, 42, 81, 95
Liquor permits, 122–23
Little Bear, 67
Little Poplar, 47
Lloyd, Reverend G.E., 137, 139
Loasby, Constable C., 51–52
Long Lake Railroad, 82
Longmore, Johnny, 55
Lucky Man's Reserve, 28

Lumsden, 141–42

M
MacDonald, A., 54, 152
Macdonald, A., store of, 34
MacDonald, Bob, 41, 49
Macdonald, Sir John A., 87
MacDowell, D.H., 69
Mackay, James, 114–15
Mackintosh, C.H., 105, 115
MacLean, W.J., 51, 53
Macleod, Judge, 105
Magrath, C.A., 101–2
Maguire, Judge, 109
Mahaffy-Clinkskill (business), 34, 45, 53
Mahaffy, Thomas E., 16
Mail, 71, 82, 87, 98, 120, 123
Mail stage, 18, 20, 33, 74, 86
Malcolm, Mr., 52
Man Without Blood, 67
Manitoba Act, 95
Manitoba School question, 115
Manitou, 70
Mann, George, 119
Marchand, Father, 45
Marcotte, Mr., 133, 144
Marquis (boat), 18
Maskell, Pat, 92–93
McCauley, M., 116
McIntosh, Robert, 141, 158
McKay, Dr. W.J., 148
McKay, James, 152
McKay, Thomas, 100
McKay, William, 34–35
McKenzie, Mr., 145
McLean, W.J., 44
McNab, A.P., 152–54
McPhail, Mr., 115–6
Mears, Mr., 71
Medicine Hat, 156
Mennonites, 5, 132
Mercer, J.B., 117–20
Middleton, General Fred, 49, 56, 58–61, 127
Miller, Captain, 57
Minto, Lord, 130
Miserable Man, 67
Mitchell, C.H., 151
Mitchell, Tom, 71, 102

Moonias (white people), 112
Moose Creek, 119
Moose Jaw, 79, 87, 94, 153
Moose Mountain, 6, 9–10, 12-3, 15
Moosomin, 10, 44
Morris, Colonel, 40, 48
Morse, Mr., 146
Mowatt, D., 95, 99–100
Mulholland, Mr., 18–19
Munroe, Dr., 150
Murray, W.C., 152, 158

N
Nash, Captain E.A., 31
Nash, Harry, 39
Neff, Mr., 84, 89, 95, 102
Nelsonville, 4, 6
Nez Perce Jack, 38–39
Nolin, Charles, 48, 96, 115
Norman, Leonard, 131
North Battleford, 129
North Qu'Appelle, 100
North Saskatchewan River, 34, 97–98, 104, 118, 127–28, 143
North West (steamer), 127
North West Acts, 90
North West Council, 75, 79
North West Territories Act, The, 75, 79–80, 90, 94, 102, 116
North-West Mounted Police, 23, 25, 34, 38, 64, 68–70, 103, 118, 121, 123, 126, 131
   and Election of 1886, 78–79, 81–82
   and Indians, 28–29, 44, 46–7, 49–50, 53–54, 56, 62
North-West Mounted Police stores, 36, 40

O
Oak Lake, 7, 157
Oliver, Frank R., 81, 89, 106–7, 111, 116, 146
Onion Lake, 45, 108–9, 114, 119
Ontario Act, 95
Osler settlement, 132
Ottawa Foot Guards, 54
Otter Station, 72, 74, 86
Otter, Colonel, 49, 54, 56–57

P
Palmer House, 26

Parisian (ship), 2
Payne, James, 27, 41, 60, 67
Pemmican, 71, 88
Pipestone Creek, 6, 10, 14–15
Poitras, Joe, 48
Portage la Prairie, 4, 150
Poundmaker, 36, 56, 59–61, 68–69
Poundmaker's Reserve, 28, 31, 35, 41, 47
Pow-wow, 29
Presbyterian Home Missions, 29
Price, Ben, 108
Price, Joe, 39
Price, Mrs. Joe, 39
Primeau, Mr., 48
Prince Albert, 16–20, 22–24, 33, 48, 58, 69,
  82, 84, 87–88, 115–16, 118, 123, 125–26,
  130, 141, 144, 150, 153, 158
Prince Brothers, 104
Prince, B., 133, 137
Princess (steamer), 16
Pritchard, John, 45
Prohibition days, 93
Public schools, 107
Public Service, 80, 123
Public utilities, 144

Q
Qu-Appelle, 10, 16, 153
Qu'Appelle, Long Lake and Saskatchewan
  Railway, 82, 87, 144, 151
Qu-Appelle station, 82
Qu-Appelle valley, 26, 141
Queen's Own Rifles, The, 54–55, 58
Quinn, Henry, 44–45
Quinn, Thomas, 45, 67

R
Rae, J.M., 34–35
Railway, 87, 103, 112, 115, 123, 125, 139,
  141, 143
Ranching, 99, 103
Rapid City, 4
Reaman, Joel, 100–01
Rebellion of 1885, 21–22, 31, 61–62, 104,
  111
Red Berry Lake, 128
Red Deer, 84
Red Fox, 121
Red River, 6, 16

Red River carts, 9, 33
Red River Jig, 25
Reed, Haytor, 60
Regina, 21, 23, 26, 68, 82, 84, 93, 95, 113,
  141–2, 146–7, 152–4
Regina, Long Lake and Saskatoon Railway,
  82
Remedial Bill, 115
Richardson, B.P., 84
Richardson, Hugh, 49
Richardson, Judge, 79, 104, 123
Riel, Louis, 22, 31, 48, 59, 61, 96
Riversdale, 140, 144
Roberts Company, 159
Robertson, Rev. James (Lang Jamie), 29
Roman Catholic Mission, 27, 34, 45, 68
Roman Catholic schools, 106, 107
Roman Catholic voters, 108,
Roman Catholics, 109–10
Rose, E., 118
Rose, J., 118
Ross, Charlie, 53
Ross, Dan, 30, 41, 49
Ross, James H., 79, 81, 94, 100, 113
Rosthern, 131–5, 147
Rouleau, Dr., 34, 42
Rouleau, Judge, 34–5, 42, 54
Round The Sky, 67
Royal, Joseph, 79–82, 96, 101, 105
Russell House, 72

S
Saskatchewan district (school), 83
Saskatchewan Herald, The, 23, 65, 70, 82, 87
Saskatchewan River, 17, 24, 33, 44, 48, 55,
  67, 86
  power from, 151
Saskatchewan, University of, 140, 147, 158
colleges of, 153, 158
construction of, 155, 157
location of, 147, 153–54
  See also, University, endowment of
Saskatchewan Valley Land Company, 130
Saskatoon (1885–1899), 33, 71, 73, 83,
  87–88, 93, 99, 102–3, 118, 120–23
Saskatoon (1900–1912), 125–26, 129–32,
  134–39, 141–47, 149–53, 156–58
Saskatoon Phoenix, 131, 135, 140, 143,
  146–49

Saskatoon school board, 140
Saskatoon Trail, 110
Sautmarket, 114
School Ordinance, 79
Schools ordinance, 106
Scott, W.J., 34, 38, 103
Selkirk, 16, 18
Seneca root, 113–34
Separate Schools, 91, 95–96, 106–7
Sewage disposal plant, 161
Sewerage system, 149, 150
Sifton, Clifford, 106
Sign language (with Doukhobors), 128
Sillers, George, 131
Sinclair, W.H., 131
Sixty Mile Bush Station, 73
Skelton, J.M., 77, 91, 109, 117–18
Smart, Frank, 41, 49, 53
Smith, D.T., 148–49
Smith, J.A., 141, 148
South Saskatchewan River, 19, 41, 48, 66, 71
Speers, Superintendent, 136–8
Squaws, 4, 29, 58
St. Albert, 119
St. Paul and Manitoba Railway, 3
St. Paul, 2–3
St. Paul's church, 158
Steward, Dr. P.D., 131
Stoney Reserve, 30, 38, 67
Stonies (Indians), 29, 41, 48
Storer, Henry, 49
Sutherland, William C., 100–01, 141, 148
Swift Creek, 12
Swift Current, 23, 25–26, 30, 35, 40–41, 44, 49, 53, 57, 66, 67, 71, 74, 86, 127

T
Taylor, Dora Babington (Clinkskill's wife), 16
Taylor settlement, 47
Telegraph communication, 44, 87, 93, 109, 119
Temperance Colonization Society, 125, 140
Thompson, James H., 149
Thompson, Levi, 152
Thorburn, Mr., 84
Thunderchild's band, 44
Tobacco, 16, 29, 36, 40, 42, 57

Tobacco Creek, 68
Touchwood district, 19, 26
Treaty money, 28
Tremont, Bernard, 67
Troy, 16, 18, 25–26
Turner, Bill, 53
Turriff, Mr., 81
Turtle River, 44
Tweed, T., 84, 89, 95, 102, 113
Typhoid fever epidemic (1886), 68

U
University, endowment of, 85
University of Saskatchewan Act, The, 152

W
Wall, Mr., 98
Wallis Chipman, 149, 159
Wallis, W.R.C., 141
Wandering Spirit, 67
Warman, 144
West Lyne, 4
West Saskatoon, 130
Western Hotel, 157
Wetmore, E.L., 157
White people, 21, 35, 41, 49–50, 71, 112, 121
White, Constable, 53
Whitewood district, 107
Williscraft, John, 27, 45
Willoughby, Dr. J.H.C., 131–32, 140
Wilson, H.C., 79
Wilson, James R., 126, 141, 148, 155
Windsor Hotel, 88
Winnipeg Oil Company, 158
Wolseley, 84
Wright, Mr., 44
Wyld, Robert, 38, 103

Y
Young & Brown, 131
Young, Mr., 140